John Jenkins is an Australian editor, journalist and poet. The author of two books on contemporary music and several books of poetry, he has also written widely for newspapers and magazines.

TRAVELERS' TALES

OF OLD CUBA

EDITED BY JOHN JENKINS

OCEAN PRESS
Melbourne • New York

www.oceanbooks.com.au

ISBN 1-876175-37-0

First printed 2002

Printed in Australia by McPherson's Printing Group

Library of Congress Control Number: 2001098633

Published by Ocean Press
Australia: GPO Box 3279, Melbourne, Victoria 3001, Australia
    ●Fax: (61-3) 9329 5040   ●Tel: (61-3) 9326 4280
    ●E-mail: info@oceanbooks.com.au
USA: PO Box 1186 Old Chelsea Station, New York, NY 10113-1186, USA
    ●Tel: (718) 246-4160

OCEAN PRESS DISTRIBUTORS
United States and Canada: LPC Group,
    22 Broad St, #34, Milford, CT 06460, USA
Britain and Europe: Global Book Marketing,
    38 King Street, London, WC2E 8JT, UK
Australia and New Zealand: Astam Books,
    57-61 John Street, Leichhardt, NSW 2040, Australia
Cuba and Latin America: Ocean Press,
    Calle 21 #406, Vedado, Havana, Cuba

www.oceanbooks.com.au

contents

introduction

There are few places in the world as colorful and interesting as Cuba, and today the island continues to hold the same allure for visitors that it has throughout its long and often turbulent history.

Cuba is the largest island, and Havana the largest city, in the Caribbean. Indeed, Havana is one of the oldest and finest cities in the Americas. Founded in the second decade of the 16th century, then fortified against pirates by a succession of military governors, the port of Havana sheltered flotillas of Spanish treasure ships, and became the gateway of the Spanish empire in the New World.

In recognition of its rich architectural and historical legacy, the old quarter of Havana (*La Habana Vieja*) was declared a UNESCO World Heritage Site in 1982.

Many of the places you will read about in these pages can still be seen today, magnificently evoking the romance and drama — as well as darker episodes of slavery and tyranny — that are all part of the island's colorful past.

Many pieces in this selection were written by American visitors to Cuba, as Americans and Cubans have long been involved in a complex love/hate relationship, which continues to the present.

While Cubans in the mid-19th century might have clamored for independence from Spain, it was often difficult for the "gringos" to understand that this did not mean swapping one form of economic and cultural subjugation for another, nor the island becoming a mere protectorate of its giant neighbor to the north.

American interests were to the fore in Cuba even before invading American forces routed the Spanish near Santiago de Cuba in 1898. And the "American era" — when planters, industrialists and investors made their fortunes in Cuba, and the island was turned into a glittering Caribbean tourist paradise for boat-rail commuters from Miami — continued late into the 1950s.

But this selection of travelers' tales is not meant as a history — and even less as a political primer. Nevertheless, I hope it *does* convey to the reader some sense of the grand sweep of life in old Cuba, from its "discovery" by Columbus in 1492 until the collapse of the infamous and corrupt Batista regime with the revolution in 1958-59.

Good travelers' stories should not only inform, but should also remain "a good read," firing the imagination. Alternatively, they must provide interesting first-hand insights into the ongoing festival of daily life. And all, ideally, should be full of the flavor, detail and manners of the era to which they belong.

Certainly, good stories were not hard to find — as you would expect from a country as various as Cuba. And the subjects tackled by our travelers who write, and writers who travel, are wonderfully diverse. Topics include the old days of the buccaneers; the slave era; the sugar and cigar trade; Cuban home life; smugglers; Afro-Cuban rites; the wars of independence; filibusters and banana barons; the spectacle of carnival time; Cuban night life; the Mafia in Havana and much more.

I hope modern visitors to Cuba have a strong sense of personal engagement with these highly literate travelers from the past, and are able to see Cuba through their eyes. In this way, the past is brought vividly back to life, and one can retrace its continuity with the present.

Finally, readers may share with these astute — and often opinionated — observers from several centuries, the emotions that stir in us all: the curiosity and excitement of discovering one of the most fascinating islands on earth.

I would like to thank Deborah Shnookal and David Deutschmann for their advice with this book.

John Jenkins

publisher's note

The publishers in no way endorse the racist or sexist language and/or viewpoints expressed by the contributors to this collection.

Original spelling and style of the pieces has been maintained.

Alexander O. Exquemelin

The Invasion of Puerto del Principe

Morgan attempts to keep St Catalina as a stronghold for the buccaneers, but fails. A description of Cuba. The invasion and capture of Puerto del Principe.

On the death of Mansveldt, his old admiral, Morgan himself would gladly have kept St Catalina as a robbers' eyrie, having used the island on various occasions as a rendezvous with his comrades. He was constantly looking for means of putting this plan into effect, and had written to various merchants in New England to send out supplies to the island. In time, he intended to have made St Catalina so strong it would have been impossible for the Spaniards to oust him, nor would the might of the King of England have been able to do much damage to his position. His schemes came to nothing, however, when the island was lost to the Spaniards.

Morgan refused to be daunted, but on the contrary began setting new plans afoot. He equipped a ship, resolving to make up a fleet of as many buccaneers as he could bring together in order to launch an attack on some important city in the Spanish dominions. He gave his fellow rovers a rendezvous in the South Cays of Cuba, where the fleet could assemble and at once consider where to attack. So that my readers may fully understand this account, I shall first give a brief description of the island.

Cuba lies between latitudes 20 and 23° north, extending 160 leagues from east to west, and 40 leagues in width. It is no less fruitful than Hispaniola, and exports an immense quantity of hides, known in Europe as Havana hides. Cuba is surrounded by innumerable small islands, known as Cays, frequently used by the buccaneers as bases from which to harry the Spaniards.

The island has several fine rivers and some excellent ports. In the south are St Jago, St Maria, Espiritu Santo, Trinidad, Xagua, Cabo de Corrientes and more besides, while on the north side lie Havana, Puerto Mariano, Santa Cruz, Mataricos, Puerto del Principe and Baracao. St Jago is the capital of half the island, and has a resident governor and a bishop. Most of its commerce is with the Canary Islands, where it sends sugar, tobacco and hides from its subordinate towns. Although protected by a fort, this city has been plundered by buccaneers from Jamaica and Tortuga.

Havana, the capital of the western part of the island, is one of the strongest and most famous cities in all the West Indies. Its major export is excellent tobacco, with which it supplies all New Spain and Costa Rica, as far as the South Sea. Havana is defended by three strong forts — two in the port, and one on a hill commanding the town. There are more than 10,000 inhabitants, the merchants trading with New Spain, Campeche, Honduras and Florida. All the ships from New Spain, Caracas, Cartagena, Costa Rica and Honduras call in there to take on fresh supplies on their way to Spain, since it lies on their route. The silver fleet always calls in there, to complete its cargo with hides and logwood.

Morgan had hardly been two months in the South Cays of Cuba before he had assembled a fleet of some 12 vessels, with 700 men, both English and French. He called a general council to decide where they should attack. Some proposed a surprise assault by night on Havana itself, saying they could easily plunder the city and carry off some of the priests as prisoners before the forts were ready to put up any defence. Everyone gave his opinion on this proposal, but it was not carried. Some of the men had been prisoners in Havana, and they declared the buccaneers were not yet strong enough to plunder the city. If they could form a fleet of 1,500 men, then there would be a good chance of taking Havana. In that case, the ships could be anchored off the Island of Pines and the men sent upriver in small boats to Matamano, only 14 leagues from Havana. However, as the buccaneers had no means of getting together such a force, they resolved to attack elsewhere.

Another man proposed an assault on Puerto del Principe. He had been there, he said, and there was plenty of money in the town, for it was where the Havana merchants came to buy hides. Lying at some distance from the sea, the place had never been plundered, so the inhabitants had no fear of the English.

This proposal was considered and agreed upon, and Morgan at once ordered his fleet to weigh anchor and set sail for the port of St Maria, the nearest place to Puerto del Principe. Before they reached this destination a Spaniard, who had long been a prisoner in the hands of the English and had picked up some words of their language, overheard the buccaneers muttering about Puerto del Principe. This man jumped overboard one night and began swimming for the nearest island. The English at once sprang into their canoes to fish him out again, but he managed to land before they could catch him and hid among the trees, where they could not find him.

Next day this Spaniard swam from one islet to the next till he reached the Cuban coast. He was familiar with the roads and before long arrived at Puerto del Principe, where he warned the inhabitants of the corsairs' approach and the forces at their disposal. The Spaniards immediately began hiding their goods, while the governor assembled all the men he could, including a number of slaves. He had a great number of trees felled to block the road and laid various ambushes, mounted with cannon. About 800 men were mustered, both from the town itself and from neighbouring places. Having manned the ambuscades with as many as he judged necessary, the governor kept the main body of defenders in an open field near the city, whence he could see the enemy's approach from afar.

The Spaniards were still busy equipping their ambuscades when the buccaneers came upon them unawares. Finding the road blocked, they had made their way through the woods, thus avoiding several of the traps set for them. At length they reached the open field, or *savana* as the Spanish call it. The governor, thinking the enemy would be full of fear when they saw the numerous forces he had gathered to resist them, instantly despatched a troop of horsemen to take them from the rear and cut them down as they fled. But events fell out otherwise.

The buccaneers, who had been advancing all this time with drums beating and banners flying, now began to spread out in a half-moon and at the same time to fall upon the Spaniards, who at first resisted them fiercely — but the battle did not last for long. The buccaneers never missed their mark, and kept up a continuous fire without pausing in their charge. The defenders' courage began to flag, especially when they saw their governor fall. They began to retreat towards the forest, where they would have a better chance of escape, but most of them were struck down before they reached shelter, although some finally did escape in the woods.

The buccaneers now made their way towards the town, victors of the field and full of high spirits, for although the battle on the *savana* had lasted four hours, they had suffered few casualties. Soon they entered the town, where they encountered fresh resistance from a group who had stayed there with the women, helped by some who had taken part in the battle on the *savana* and still hoped to prevent the enemy from plundering the town. Some locked themselves in their houses and fired from the windows, but once the buccaneers became aware of this sniping they threatened to burn down the whole town, destroying women and children and all. The Spaniards then surrendered, fearing these menaces would be put into effect, and believing the rovers would be unable to hold the town under subjection for long.

The buccaneers shut up the Spaniards, including women and children and slaves, in the church, and collected all the loot they could find in the town. When this was done, they began to go out on marauding expeditions, every day bringing back fresh booty and prisoners, so time did not lie heavy on their hands. In fact, they led a life after their own hearts, eating and drinking so long as there was anything to find. But time did not pass so lightly for the poor wretched prisoners in the church, living in fear. They were given little to eat, and every day were pained and plagued by unspeakable tortures to make them say where they had hidden money or goods. Many a poor man was tortured who had neither, who earned only enough by his daily labour to support his wife and family. It made no difference to these tyrants, who said, "If he won't confess, string him up." There were poor women with babies at their breast and no nourishment to give these innocents, for the mothers themselves were dying of hunger and discomfort, but neither did their plight rouse any compassion in the buccaneers. When they felt like it, they would shoot a cow or bull and, having helped themselves to the best meat, would give the remains to the prisoners, who could do what they pleased with it.

But when there was nothing more to eat or to drink or to plunder, the buccaneers decided to take their leave. They informed the prisoners that money must be found for their ransom or otherwise they would be transported to Jamaica, and also that they must pay a ransom for the city, or the rovers would burn it to ashes before they left. They sent out four of the Spanish prisoners to collect this tribute, and to speed up the payment subjected the rest to further torments.

The four Spaniards returned, and went lamenting to Morgan, the general of the buccaneers, saying they had done their best to get hold of ransom money but they had been unable to find any of the people in hiding. If he would only wait another fortnight, they were sure the money he demanded could be collected. While they were busy negotiating with Morgan about the ransom, seven or eight buccaneers, who had been out of town shooting cattle, returned with a Negro prisoner. This man had been carrying letters meant for some of the prisoners. These were opened, and proved to be from the governor of St Jago, saying he would soon be coming to relieve the town, and telling them not to be too hasty in paying any ransom or levy. They must delay matters for another fortnight if possible, giving the buccaneers hope that the money would then be paid.

Seeing the Spaniards intended to play him false, Morgan had all the plunder instantly carried to the shore where his ships lay, and announced that unless the ransom was paid next day he would set the town on fire. He said nothing about the letters which had come into his hands. The Spaniards again answered that it was impossible: their people were scattered here and there, and the money could not be collected in so short a time. Morgan, well aware of their secrets, then said they must send 500 cattle to the sea-shore, together with salt to preserve the meat. They agreed to this arrangement, and Morgan and the buccaneers marched down to the shore, taking six of the principal citizens as hostages, together with all the captured slaves.

Next morning the Spaniards brought the 500 beasts they had promised down to the shore where the fleet lay anchored, and asked for their hostages back again. But Morgan, who did not trust them and had no desire to fight when there was no booty to be gained from it, refused to give up his prisoners before all the meat was on board. The Spaniards, in order to release their fellow-citizens and leaders with all speed, helped the buccaneers to slaughter the animals and salt the flesh. The buccaneers gladly let them do this work, which left them with scarcely anything to do but carry the meat on board.

In the meantime, trouble broke out between the French and the English because an Englishman had shot a Frenchman dead on account of a marrow-bone. I have recounted earlier how the *boucaniers,* when they have killed a beast, suck out the marrow, and these men did the same thing. The Frenchman had flayed an animal and the Englishman came up and helped himself to the marrow-bones. This started the quarrel, and they challenged each other to fight it out with muskets. On coming to the duelling place, away from the rest, the Englishman was ready before the other, and shot him through the body from behind. Upon this, the French seized their muskets and wanted to fall on the English, but Morgan thrust himself between the rival groups and promised the French he would do right by them and have the Englishman hanged as soon as they reached Jamaica.

The man would have had no blame if he had not shot his opponent treacherously, for duels are a daily occurrence among the buccaneers — but they have to be fought fairly. When a man kills his opponent in fair fight, no more questions are asked. Morgan had the criminal bound hand and foot, to take him along to Jamaica.

Meanwhile the meat had been salted and loaded in the ships, and then Morgan handed over the hostages and his fleet set sail. He had given each ship a rendezvous on one of the islands, where they could share out the spoils. On arrival, they found this amounted to some 50,000 pieces of eight in ready money, silverwork and the various other goods they had pillaged. They had hoped for greater booty: this amount was of little help to them, for it would not even pay the debts they owed in Jamaica.

Morgan proposed going to plunder some other place before returning to Jamaica, but the French could not agree with the English and went their own way, leaving Morgan with only his own people.

He had pointed out to the French that he would have been very glad of their company, and had promised to give them protection, but they did not wish to stay. Nevertheless, they parted good friends, and Morgan promised he would have justice done on behalf of their comrade who had been shot. This he did, for as soon as he arrived at Jamaica he had the treacherous duellist instantly hanged.

Maturin M. Ballou

The Aborigines of Cuba; A Slave Ship; Marti the Smuggler, circa 1854

The Aborigines of Cuba

The native Cubans were of tawny complexion and beardless, resembling in many respects the aborigines of North America, and as Columbus described them in his first communication to his royal patrons, were "loving, tractable, and peaceable; though entirely naked, their manners were decorous and praise-worthy." The wonderful fecundity of the soil, its range of noble mountains, its widespread and well-watered plains, with its extended coast line and excellent harbors, all challenged the admiration of the discoverers, so that Columbus recorded in his journal these words: "It is the most beautiful island that eyes ever beheld, — full of excellent ports and profound rivers." And again he says; "It excels all other countries, as far as the day surpasses the night in brightness and splendor." The spot where the Spaniards first landed is supposed to be on the east coast, just west of Nuevitas. "As he approached the island," says Irving, "he was struck with its magnitude and the grandeur of its features: its airy mountains, which reminded him of Sicily; its fertile valleys and long sweeping plains, watered by noble rivers; its stately forests; its bold promontories and stretching headlands, which melted away into remotest distance."

Excursions inland corroborated the favorable impression made by the country bordering upon the coast. The abundance of yams, Indian corn, and various fruits, together with the plentifulness of wild cotton, impressed the explorers most favorably. Their avarice and greed were also stimulated by the belief that gold was to be found in large quantities, having received enough to convince them of its actual presence in the soil; but in the supposition that the precious metal was to be found in what is termed paying quantities they were mistaken.

The Spaniards were not a little surprised to see the natives using rude pipes, in which they smoked a certain dried leaf with apparent gratification. Tobacco was indigenous, and in the use of this now universal narcotic, these simple savages indulged in at least one luxury. The flora was strongly individualized. The frangipanni, tall and almost leafless, with thick fleshy shoots, decked with a small white blossom, was very fragrant and abundant; here also was the wild passion-flower, in which the Spaniards thought they beheld the emblems of our Saviour's passion... Here the invaders also observed and noted the night-blooming cereus. They were delighted by fruits of which they knew not the names, such as the custard-apple, mango, zapota, banana, and others, growing in such rank luxuriance as to seem miraculous...

The inoffensive, unsuspicious natives shared freely everything they possessed with the invaders. Hospitality was with them an instinct, fostered by nature all about them; besides which it was a considerable time before they ceased to believe their guests superior beings descended from the clouds in their winged vessels. The Indians lived in villages of 200 or 300 houses, built of wood and palm-leaf, each dwelling containing several families, the whole of one lineage, and all were governed by caciques or kings, the spirit of the government being patriarchal.

We are told by Las Casas, who accompanied Velasquez in all his expeditions, that "their dances were graceful and their singing melodious, while with primeval innocence they thought no harm of being clad only with nature's covering." The description of the gorgeous hospitality extended to these treacherous invaders is absolutely touching in the light of our subsequent knowledge. They reared no sacred temples, nor did they seem to worship idols, and yet some few antiquities have been preserved which would seem to indicate that the natives possessed grotesque images, half human and half animal... According to Las Casas, the native Cubans had a vague tradition of the formation of the earth, and of all created things; of the deluge, of the ark, the raven, and the dove. They knew the tradition of Noah also, according to the same high authority, but for our own part we do not believe that the aborigines had any knowledge of this Biblical story. Their priests were fanatics and kept the people in fear by gross and extravagant means; but as to any formulated system of religious worship, it may be doubted if the aborigines of Cuba recognized any at the time of its discovery by Columbus. (The island of Cuba was discovered by the great Genoese pilot, on the 28th day of October, 1492.) Unbroken peace reigned among them, and they turned their hands against no other people.

These aborigines exhibited many of the traits universally evinced by savage races, such as painting their bodies with red earth and adorning their heads with the feathers of brilliant birds. Much of the soil is red, almost equal to a pigment, for which purpose it was employed by the natives. They lived mostly in the open air, weaving themselves hammocks in which they slept, suspended among the trees. The cotton which they spun grew wild, but tobacco they planted and cultivated after a rude fashion. The iguana and the voiceless dog... were hunted and eaten, the former of the lizard family, the latter scarcely more than 15 inches long. They had domestic birds which they fattened and ate. Their only arms were lances tipped with sea-shells, and a sort of wooden sword, both of which were more for display than for use. Fish they caught in nets and also with hooks made of bones. Their boats, or canoes, were formed of the dug-out trunks of trees, and some of these canoes, as Columbus tells us, were sufficiently large to accommodate 50 men...

History has preserved a remarkable and characteristic speech made by a venerable cacique, who approached Columbus with great reverence on the occasion of his second visit to Cuba, and who, after presenting him with a basket of ripe fruit, said: "Whether you are divinities or mortal men, we know not. You have come into these countries with a force, against which, were we inclined to resist, it would be folly. We are all therefore at your mercy; but if you are men, subject to mortality like ourselves, you cannot be unapprised that after this life there is another, wherein a very different portion is allotted to good and bad men. If therefore you expect to die, and believe, with us, that every one is to be rewarded in a future state according to his conduct in the present, you will do no hurt to those who do none to you." This was duly interpreted to Columbus by a native whom he had taken to Spain, and who had there acquired the Spanish language. His name was Didacus, and the date of the speech was July 7, 1492. The truth of this version is attested by Herrera and others.

The reception which Bartholomew Columbus, who was appointed deputy governor in the absence of the Admiral, afterwards met with in his progress through the island to collect tribute from the several caciques manifested not only kindness and submission, but also munificence. Having heard of the eagerness of the strangers for gold, such of them as possessed any brought it forth and freely bestowed it upon the Spaniards. Those who had not gold brought abundance of cotton. One cacique in the interior, named Behechio, invited the deputy governor to a state entertainment, on which occasion he was received with great ceremony. As he approached the king's dwelling, the royal wives, 30 in number, carrying branches of palm in their hands, came forth to greet the guest with song and dance. These matrons were succeeded by a train of virgins. The first wore aprons of cotton, the last were arrayed only in the innocence of nature, their hair flowing long and freely about their shoulders and necks. Their limbs were finely proportioned, and their complexions, though brown, were smooth, shining, and lovely. The Spaniards were struck with admiration, believing that they beheld the dryads of the woods and the nymphs of the ancient fables. The branches which they bore were delivered to the strangers with low obeisance, indicating entire submission. When the Spaniards entered the rural palace, amid songs and the rude music of the people, they found there a plentiful and, according to the Indian mode of living, a sumptuous banquet prepared for them.

After the repast the guests were each conducted to separate lodgings, and each provided with a cotton hammock. On the next day feasting and games were resumed; dancing and singing closed each evening for four consecutive days, and when the deputy governor and his people departed, they were laden with gifts by their generous entertainers, who also accompanied them far on their way. This episode will perhaps serve better to give us a just insight into the condition and character of the aborigines of Cuba at that early period than any amount of detailed description possibly could.

These aborigines, according to Las Casas, had no tradition, even touching their own origin, and when asked about it only shook their heads and pointed to the sky. Antiquarians have endeavored to draw some reliable or at least reasonable deductions from the collection of bones and skeletons found in the mountain caves of the island, but no conclusion worthy of record has ever been arrived at...

During the 10 years subsequent to its discovery, Columbus visited and partially explored the island at four different times, the last being in 1502, four years previous to his death, which took place at Valladolid in 1506. It seems singular to us that his investigations left him still ignorant of the fact that Cuba was an island and not a part of a new continent. This conviction remained with him during his lifetime. It was not until 1511 that the Spaniards commenced to colonize the island, when Diego Columbus, then governor of San Domingo, sent an expedition of 300 men for the purpose, under the command of Diego Velasquez, whose landing was disputed by the natives. A period of 10 years had served to open their eyes to Spanish lust and love of gold, and from having at first regarded them as superior beings, entitled to their obedience, they were finally thus driven to fight them in self-defense. But what could naked savages, armed only with clubs and spears, accomplish against Europeans, trained soldiers, furnished with firearms, protected by plate armor, and accompanied by bloodhounds — men who had learned the art of war by fighting successfully with the valiant Moors? The natives were at once overpowered and hundreds were slaughtered. From that time forth they became the slaves of their conquerors...

Diego Velasquez, the earliest governor of the island, appears to have been an energetic and efficient magistrate, and to have administered affairs with vigor and intelligence. He did not live, however, in a period when justice ever erred on the side of mercy, and his harsh and cruel treatment of the aborigines will always remain a stain upon his memory. The native population soon dwindled away under the sway of the Spaniards, who imposed tasks upon them far beyond their physical powers of endurance. The victims of this hardship had no one to befriend them at that time, and no one has done them justice in history. The few glimpses of their character which have come down to us are of a nature greatly to interest us in this now extinct race. Their one fault was in trusting the invaders at all. At the outset they could have swept them from the face of the earth, but, once permitted to establish themselves, they soon became too powerful to be driven out of the land. A native chief, whose only crime was that of taking up arms in defense of the integrity of his little territory, fell into the hands of Velasquez, and was cruelly burned at the stake, near what is now the town of Yara, as a punishment for his patriotism. The words of this unfortunate but brave chief (Hatuey), extorted by the torments which he suffered, were: "I prefer hell to heaven, if there are Spaniards in heaven!"

In point of energetic action and material progress, Velasquez reminds us of a later governor-general, the famous Tacon. In a single decade, Velasquez founded the seven cities of Baracoa, Santiago de Cuba, Trinidad, Bayamo, Puerto del Principe, St. Spiritus, and, on the south coast near Batabano, Havana, since removed to its present site. He caused the mines to be opened and rendered them profitable, introduced valuable breeds of cattle, instituted agricultural enterprise, and opened a large trade with San Domingo, Jamaica, and the Spanish peninsula. Population increased rapidly, thousands of persons emigrating annually from Europe, tempted by the inviting stories of the returned explorers. Emigration schemes were approved and fostered by the home government, and thus a large community was rapidly divided among the several cities upon the island. Still this new province was considered mainly in the light of a military depot by the Spanish throne, in its famous operations at that period in Mexico. The fact that it was destined to prove the richest jewel in the Castilian crown, and a mine of wealth to the Spanish treasury, was not dreamed of at that date in its history. Even the enthusiastic followers of Cortez, who sought that fabulous El Dorado in the New World, had no promise for this gem of the Caribbean Sea; but, in spite of every side issue and all contending interests, the island continued to grow in numbers and importance, while its native resources were far beyond the appreciation of the home government.

Thus Cuba became the headquarters of the Spanish power in the West, forming the point of departure for those military expeditions which, though circumscribed in numbers, were yet so formidable in the energy of the leaders, and in the arms, discipline, courage, fanaticism, and avarice of their followers, that they were amply adequate to carry out the vast scheme of conquest for which they were designed… giving Spain a colonial empire far more splendid than that of any other power in Christendom.

A Slave Ship

The author's first visit to the island of Cuba was during the year 1845, at a period when the slave traffic was vigorously, though surreptitiously, carried on between Africa and the island. The trade was continued so late as 1853, and occasional cargoes were brought over even later, slavers having been captured on the south coast two years subsequent to the last named date. The slave vessels generally sought a landing on the south side, both as being nearest and safest for them, but when they were hard pressed they made a port wherever it could be most easily reached. A favorite point at the time of which we speak, was in the Bay of Broa, on the south coast, nearly opposite to the Isle of Pines. It was here in 1845 that the author witnessed a scene which forms the theme of the following chapter…

We were on a brief visit to the coffee estate of Don Herero, near Guinea, and having expressed a desire to visit the southern coast, our host proposed that we should do so together on the following day. We were to start on horseback quite early in the morning, so as to accomplish the distance before the heat of the sun should become oppressive…

As we rode off that delicious morning towards our destination, mounted upon a couple of bright little easy-going Cuban ponies, with their manes and tails roached (that is, trimmed closely, after a South American fashion), the cool, fresh air was as stimulating as wine…

A ride of a couple of leagues or more brought us finally to a gentle rise of ground, which opened to our view the ocean, and a line of coast extending for many miles east and west. It was still quite early, and a morning mist hung over the quiet Caribbean Sea, which stretches away southward towards the Isle of Pines and the more distant isle of Jamaica. A gentle breeze began at that moment to disperse the mist and gradually in conjunction with the sun to lift the veil from the face of the waters... Presently the indistinct outline of a graceful tracery of spars and cordage greeted the eye through the misty gauze, growing steadily more and more distinct and gradually descending towards the sea level, until at last there lay before us in full view, with a look of treacherous tranquillity, the dark, low hull of a brigantine.

"A slaver!" was the mutual and simultaneous exclamation which burst from our lips as we gazed intently on the small but symmetrical vessel.

Don Herero looked particularly intelligent, but said nothing. There could be no doubt as to the trade which engaged such a clipper craft. No legitimate commerce was suggested by her appearance, no honest trade demanded such manifest sacrifice of carrying capacity. It was very natural that her guilty character should add interest to her appearance and cause us to examine her very minutely. A short distance from where we stood there was gathered a group of a dozen or more persons, who silently regarded the brigantine, but they evinced no surprise at her appearance there so close to the shore. She was of a most graceful model, perfect in every line, with bows almost as sharp as a knife. The rig was also quite unusual and entirely new to us. Her deck was flush fore and aft. Not so much as an inch of rise was allowed for a quarter-deck, a style which gave large stowage capacity below deck, the level of which came up to within a couple of feet of the cappings of the bulwarks. As we have before intimated, it required no interpreter to indicate what business the brigantine was engaged in. A single glance at her, lying in so unfrequented a place, was enough. The rakish craft was of Baltimore build, of about 200 tons measurement, and, like many another vessel turned out by the Maryland builders, was designed to make successfully the famous middle passage to or from the coast of Cuba, loaded with kidnapped negroes from the shores of Africa. The two requisites of these clippers were great speed and large stowage capacity for a human freight.

While we were exchanging some remarks upon the subject, our attention was suddenly drawn towards another striking object upon the waters of the bay.

Nearly a league beyond the slaver, looming up above the mist, we could now make out three top-masts, clearly defined, the stately set of which, with their firm and substantial rig, betrayed the fact that there floated beneath them the hull of a French or an English man-of-war, such as was commissioned at that time to cruise in these waters for the purpose of intercepting and capturing the vessels engaged in the African slave trade.

"A cruiser has scented the brigantine," said Don Herero.

"It certainly appears so," we affirmed.

"Unless there be sharp eyes on board the little craft, the cruiser will be down upon her before her people even suspect their danger."

"The brigantine can hardly escape, at any rate," we suggested.

"Don't be too sure," said Don Herero.

It was impossible for our friend to suppress the nervous anxiety which so manifestly actuated him as he viewed the new phase of affairs.

"Look! Look! "he exclaimed.

While he spoke, a drapery of snow-white canvas fell like magic from the spars of the slaver, ready to catch the first breath of the breeze which the stranger was bringing down with him, though the larger vessel was still partially wrapped in a thin bank or cloud of fog. A couple of long sweeps were rigged out of either bow of the brigantine, and her prow, which just before was heading shoreward, was swung to seaward, while her canvas was trimmed to catch the first breath of the on-coming breeze.

"This looks like business," said Don Herero with emphasis, at the same time shading his eyes with both hands to get a better view of the situation.

"Can you define the newcomer's nationality?" we asked.

"Not yet."

"See! she is now in full sight."

"French!" exclaimed Don Herero, as the tri-colors were clearly visible hanging from her peak.

"What will the cruiser do with the brigantine?" we asked.

"First catch your hare," said our friend.

Our host then explained that the slaver had evidently intended to land her cargo under cover of the night, but had been prevented by the mist from coming to anchor in time. Fog, being so seldom known on this coast, had not entered into their calculations. She had most likely felt her way towards the shore by soundings, and was waiting for full daylight when we discovered her.

While this explanation was being made, the brigantine had already got steerage way upon her, aided by the steady application of the sweeps, and her sharp bow was headed off shore. Nothing on the sea, unless it were a steamer, could hold speed with these fly-aways, which were built for just such emergencies as the present. The gradually freshening breeze had now dispersed the mist, and the two vessels were clearly in view from the shore and to each other. The remarkable interest of the scene increased with each moment. Don Herero, with all the excitability of his nationality, could hardly contain himself as he walked rapidly back and forth, always keeping his eyes towards the sea.

The cruiser had come down under an easy spread of canvas, wearing a jib, three topsails, fore, main, and mizzen, and her spanker. It did not appear as if she had any previous intimation of the presence of the slaver, but rather that she was on the watch for just such a quarry as chance had placed within reach of her guns. The moment she discovered the brigantine, and at a signal which we could not hear upon the land, a hundred dark objects peopled her shrouds and sail of spars, and sail after sail of heavy duck was rapidly dropped and sheeted home, until the mountain of canvas began to force the large hull through the water with increasing speed.

In the meantime the lesser craft had been by no means idle. In addition to the regular square and fore and aft sails of a brigantine, she had a mizzen-mast stepped well aft not more than four feet from her taffrail, upon which she had hoisted a spanker and gaff-topsail, thus completing a most graceful and effective rig, and spreading a vast amount of canvas for a vessel of her moderate tonnage. It was quite impossible to take one's eyes off the two vessels. It was a race for life with the slaver, whose people worked with good effect at the sweeps and in trimming their sails to make the most out of the light but favorable wind that was filling them. The larger vessel would have made better headway in a stiff breeze or half a gale of wind, but the present moderate breeze favored the guilty little brigantine, which was every moment forging ahead and increasing the distance between herself and her enemy.

"Do you see that commotion on the cruiser's bow?" asked our friend eagerly.

"Some men are gathered on the starboard bow," was our answer.

"Ay, and now she runs out a gun!"

That was plain enough to see. The cruiser trained a bow-chaser to bear on the slaver, and the boom of the gun came sluggishly over the sea a few seconds after the puff of smoke was seen. A quick eye could see the dash of the shot just astern of the brigantine, where it must have cast the spray over her quarter-deck. After a moment's delay, as if to get the true range, a second, third, and fourth shot followed, each ricochetting through and over the slight waves either to starboard or port of the slaver, without any apparent effect. The brigantine, still employing her sweeps, and with canvas well trimmed, took no notice of the shots.

Every time the gun was discharged on board the cruiser, it became necessary to fall off her course just a point or two in order to get a proper aim, and her captain was quick to see the disadvantage of this, as he was only assisting the slaver to widen the distance between them. It would seem to the uninitiated to be the easiest thing possible to cripple the brigantine by a few well directed shots, but when sailing in the wake of an enemy this is by no means so easily done. Besides, the distance between the two vessels, which was considerable, was momentarily increasing. Notwithstanding that the broad spread of canvas on board the slaver made her a conspicuous mark, still, so far as could be seen or judged of by her movements, she remained untouched by half a dozen shots, more or less, which the cruiser sent after her as she slipped away from her big adversary. We could even see that the sweeps were now taken in, showing that the master of the slaver considered the game to be in his own hands.

"The brigantine steers due south," said our friend, rubbing his hands together eagerly. "She will lead the Frenchman a wild goose chase among the Cayman Isles, where he will be most likely to run aground with his heavy draught of water. The sea round about for leagues is underlaid by treacherous coral reefs. We shall see, we shall see," he reiterated.

"But they must certainly have a good pilot on board the cruiser," we ventured to say.

"Undoubtedly," replied Don Herero, "but the brigantine is built with a centre-board, thus having, as it were, a portable keel, and can sail anywhere that a man could swim, while the cruiser, with all her armament, must draw nearly three fathoms. A ship will sometimes follow a chase into dangerous water."

"True," we responded, "the brigantine's safety lies in seeking shoal water."

"You are right, and that will be her game."

In half an hour both vessels were hull down in the offing, and were soon invisible from our point of view. The early ride and subsequent excitement had developed in us a healthy appetite, and we were strongly reminded of the fact that we had not breakfasted. We were near the little hamlet of Lenore, where there was a small inn, which we had passed on the way, and towards which we now turned our horses' heads. A breakfast of boiled eggs, fried plantains, and coffee was prepared for us and well served, much to our surprise, supplemented by a large dish of various fruits, ripe and delicious...

There were a dozen and more individuals in the Lenore inn who were more or less connected with the expected arrival of the slave brigantine, and the disappointment caused by the arrival upon the scene of the French cruiser had put them all in a very bad humor. Angry words were being exchanged among them in the large reception apartment, and Don Herero suggested that we should finish our cigars under an inviting shade in the rear of the posada.

At our host's suggestion a neighboring coffee plantation was visited, and its floral and vegetable beauties thoroughly enjoyed. It was in the very height of fragrance and promise, the broad expanse of the plantation, as far as the eye could extend, being in full bloom. Some hours were agreeably passed in examining the estate, the slaves' quarters, and the domestic arrangements, and also in partaking of the hospitalities of the generous owner, after which we rode back to Lenore.

"We must not miss the closing act of our little drama," said Don Herero, significantly.

"The closing act?" we inquired.

"Certainly. You do not suppose we have yet done with the brigantine?"

"Oh, the brigantine. Will she dare to return, now the cruiser has discovered her?"

"Of course she will, after dropping her pursuer. Strange that these French cruisers do not understand these things better; but so it is."

And Don Herero explained that the French cruisers watched the southern coasts of the island, while the English cruised on the northern shore, attempted to blockade it, and also cruised farther seaward, on the line between Africa and Cuba. A couple of American men-of-war, engaged in the same purpose of suppressing the slave trade, patrolled the African coast. It was nearly night before we got through our dinner at the posada. Just as we were preparing to leave the table, the landlord came in and announced to Don Herero that if we desired to witness the close of the morning's business in the bay, we must hurry up to the plateau.

We hastened to our former position, reaching it just in time to see the brigantine again rounding the headland. She now ran in close to the shore, where there seemed to be hardly water sufficient to float her, but the exactness and system which characterized her movements showed that her commander was not a stranger to the little bay in which he had brought his vessel. All was instantly bustle and activity, both on board and on shore. There were not more than 20 people to be seen at the shore, but each one knew his business, and went about it intelligently. There was no more loud talking or disputation. These men, all armed, were accustomed to this sort of thing, and had evidently been awaiting the slaver's arrival for some days. They were a rough-looking set of desperadoes, among whom we recognized several who had been at the posada.

The brigantine was quickly moored as near to the shore as possible, and a broad gangway of wood was laid from her deck to a projecting rock, over which a long line of dark objects was hurried, like a flock of sheep, and nearly as naked as when born into the world. We walked down to the landing-place, in order to get a closer view. The line of human beings who came out from below the deck of the slaver were mostly full-grown men, but occasionally a woman or a boy came out and hastened forward with the rest. As we drew nearer, one or two of the women, it was observed, had infants in their arms, little unconscious creatures, sound asleep, and so very young that they must have been born on the voyage. How the entire scene appealed to our indignation and sympathy! What misery these poor creatures must have endured, cooped up for 21 days in that circumscribed space! They were all shockingly emaciated, having sustained life on a few ounces of rice and a few gills of water daily distributed to them. The atmosphere, thoroughly poisoned when so confined, had proved fatal to a large number. As we stood there, one dark body was passed up from below the deck and quietly dropped into the bay. Life was extinct. It was quite impossible to suppress a shudder as we looked upon the disgraceful scene, which being observed Don Herero said, — "They look bad enough now, but a few days in the open air, with a plenty of fresh vegetables, fruits, and sweet water to drink, will bring them round. They will get a good bath directly at the first river they cross, which is the thing they most require."

While our friend was speaking, four tall, gaunt, fierce-looking negroes passed us, shackled two by two at the wrists. Their eyes rolled curiously about, full of wonder at all they saw, everything was to them so strange. They knew no more than children just born what was in store for them...

Hastening back to the posada, a large basket of cassava bread and an abundance of ripe bananas and oranges, with half a dozen bottles of wine, were procured. With these, carried by a couple of colored boys, we hastened back to the landing-place in time to distribute the refreshments to all the women and boys. The balance of the provisions were dealt out to the few men who had not already been hurried away from the spot...

We were told afterwards that there were about 350 of these poor creatures originally embarked, and over 300 were landed. Perhaps between 30 and 40 had died on the passage, unable to sustain life under such awful circumstances, packed, as they necessarily were, almost like herring in a box. Once a day, in fair weather, 30 or 40 at a time were permitted to pass a half hour on deck. That was all the respite from their confinement which they enjoyed during the three weeks' voyage. The horrors of the "middle passage" have not been exaggerated. "They must have lost many of their number by death, on the voyage," we suggested to Don Herero, as we observed their weak and tremulous condition.

"Doubtless," was the response.

"And what do they do in that case?"

"They have the ocean always alongside," was his significant reply.

"They throw them over as they did that body just now?" we asked.

"Exactly. And many a poor sick creature is cast into the sea before life is extinct," he continued.

"That is adding murder to piracy," was our natural and indignant rejoinder.

"Hush!" said Don Herero, "these are sensitive people, and desperate ones, as well. I should find it difficult to protect you if they were to overhear and understand such words."

We realized that his remarks were true enough. We were in a land of slavery, and that meant that everything evil was possible.

The last of the living freight had been landed, and arranged in marching trim they were turned with their faces inland, staggering as they went, their swollen and cramped limbs hardly able to sustain the weight of their bodies. They were all secured with handcuffs, 20 in a lot, between whom, — there being 10 on a side, — a pole was placed, and each was fastened by a chain running through the steel handcuffs to the pole. An armed Spaniard directed each lot. The faces of all were quite expressionless. They had just endured such horrors packed beneath the deck of the brigantine that the present change must have been welcome to them, lame as they were.

We had been so completely engaged in watching the colored gangs and in moving up to our lookout station of the early morning that our thoughts had not reverted to anything else, but as the last lot filed by there boomed over the waters of the bay the heavy report of a gun, at once calling our attention seaward. A change had come over the scene. That which has taken some space to relate had transpired with great rapidity. Night had settled over the scene, but the moon and stars were so marvelously bright as to render objects almost as plain as by day. The ocean lay like a sheet of silver, luminous with the reflected light poured upon it by the sparkling skies. Looking towards the southeast, we saw the French cruiser rounding the headland which formed the eastern arm of the little bay, and she had already sent a shot across the water aimed at the brigantine...

The brigantine had cast off her moorings and was now standing seaward, with her sails filled. We could distinctly see a quarter boat leave her side manned by some of her crew, who at once pulled towards the nearest landing. At the same time a bright blaze sprang up on board the slaver just amidships, and in a moment more it crept, like a living serpent, from shroud to shroud and from spar to spar, until the graceful brigantine was one sheet of flame! It was dazzling to look upon, even at the distance where we stood, the body of high-reaching flame being sharply defined against the background of sky and blue water.

While we watched the glowing view the cruiser cautiously changed her course and bore away, for fire was an enemy with which she could not contend. Presently there arose a shower of blazing matter heavenward, while a confused shock and a dull rumbling report filled the atmosphere, as the guilty brigantine was blown to atoms! Hemmed in as she was there could be no hope of escape. Her mission was ended, and her crew followed their usual orders, to destroy the ship rather than permit her to fall a prize to any government cruisers.

Marti the Smuggler

One of the most successful villains whose story will be written in history is a man named Marti, as well known in Cuba as the person of the governor-general himself. Formerly he was notorious as a smuggler and half pirate on the coast of the island, being a daring and accomplished leader of reckless men. At one time he bore the title of King of the Isle of Pines, where was his principal rendezvous, and from whence he dispatched his vessels, small, fleet crafts, to operate in the neighboring waters.

His story, well known in Cuba and to the home government, bears intimately upon our subject.

When Tacon landed on the island, and became governor-general, he found the revenue laws in a sad condition, as well as the internal regulations of the island; and, with a spirit of mingled justice and oppression, he determined to do something in the way of reform. (Tacon governed Cuba for four years, from 1834 to 1838.) The Spanish marine sent out to regulate the maritime matters of the island lay idly in port, the officers passing their time on shore, or in giving balls and dances on the decks of their vessels. Tacon saw that one of the first moves for him to make was to suppress the smuggling upon the coast, at all hazards; and to this end he set himself directly to work. The maritime force at his command was at once detailed upon this service, and they coasted night and day, but without the least success against the smugglers. In vain were all the vigilance and activity of Tacon and his agents — they accomplished nothing.

At last, finding that all his expeditions against them failed, partly from the adroitness and bravery of the smugglers, and partly from the want of pilots among the shoals and rocks that they frequented, a large and tempting reward was offered to any one of them who would desert from his comrades and act in this capacity on behalf of the government. At the same time, a double sum, most princely in amount, was offered for the person of one Marti, dead or alive, who was known to be the leader of the lawless rovers who thus defied the government. These rewards were freely promulgated, and posted so as to reach the ears and eyes of those whom they concerned; but even these seemed to produce no effect, and the government officers were at a loss how to proceed in the matter.

It was a dark, cloudy night in Havana, some three or four months subsequent to the issuing of these placards announcing the rewards as referred to, when two sentinels were pacing backwards and forwards before the main entrance to the governor's palace, just opposite the grand plaza. A little before midnight, a man, wrapped in a cloak, was watching them from behind the statue of Ferdinand, near the fountain, and, after observing that the two soldiers acting as sentinels paced their brief walk so as to meet each other, and then turn their backs as they separated, leaving a brief moment in the interval when the eyes of both were turned away from the entrance they were placed to guard, seemed to calculate upon passing them unobserved. It was an exceedingly delicate manoeuver, and required great care and dexterity to effect it; but, at last, it was adroitly done, and the stranger sprang lightly through the entrance, secreting himself behind one of the pillars in the inner court of the palace. The sentinels paced on undisturbed.

The figure which had thus stealthily effected an entrance, now sought the broad stairs that led to the governor's suite of apartments, with a confidence that evinced a perfect knowledge of the place. A second guardpost was to be passed at the head of the stairs; but, assuming an air of authority, the stranger offered a cold military salute and pressed forward, as though there was not the most distant question of his right so to do; and thus avoiding all suspicion in the guard's mind, he boldly entered the governor's reception room unchallenged, and closed the door behind him. In a large easy chair sat the commander-in-chief busily engaged in writing, but alone. An expression of undisguised satisfaction passed across the weather-beaten countenance of the newcomer at this state of affairs, as he coolly cast off his cloak and tossed it over his arm, and then proceeded to wipe the perspiration from his face. The governor, looking up with surprise, fixed his keen eyes upon the intruder — "Who enters here, unannounced, at this hour?" he asked, sternly, while he regarded the stranger earnestly.

"One who has information of value for the governor-general. You are Tacon, I suppose?"

"I am. What would you with me? Or, rather, how did you pass my guard unchallenged?"

"Of that anon, Excellency, you have offered a handsome reward for information concerning the rovers of the gulf?"

"Ha! Yes. What of them?" said Tacon, with undisguised interest.

"Excellency, I must speak with caution," continued the newcomer, "otherwise I may condemn and sacrifice myself."

"You have naught to fear on that head. The offer of reward for evidence against the scapegraces also vouchsafes a pardon to the informant. You may speak on, without fear for yourself, even though you may be one of the very confederation itself."

"You offer a reward, also, in addition, for the discovery of Marti — Captain Marti, of the smugglers — do you not?"

"We do, and will gladly make good the promise of reward for any and all information upon the subject," replied Tacon.

"First, Excellency, do you give me your knightly word that you will grant a free pardon to *me* if I reveal all that you require to know, even embracing the most secret hiding-places of the rovers?"

"I pledge you my word of honor," said the commander.

"No matter how heinous in the sight of the law my offences may have been, still you will pardon me, under the king's seal?"

"I will, if you reveal truly and to any good purpose," answered Tacon, weighing in his mind the purpose of all this precaution.

"Even if I were a leader among the rovers, myself?"

The governor hesitated for a moment, canvassing in a single glance the subject before him, and then said:

"Even then, be you whom you may; if you are able and will honestly pilot our ships and reveal the secrets of Marti and his followers, you shall be rewarded as our proffer sets forth, and yourself receive a free pardon."

"Excellency, I think I know your character well enough to trust you, else I should not have ventured here."

"Speak then; my time is precious," was the impatient reply of Tacon.

"Then, Excellency, the man for whom you have offered the largest reward, dead or alive, is now before you!"

"And you are — Marti!"

The governor-general drew back in astonishment, and cast his eyes towards a brace of pistols that lay within reach of his right hand; but it was only for a single moment, when he again assumed entire self-control, and said, "I shall keep my promise, sir, provided you are faithful, though the laws call loudly for your punishment, and even now you are in my power. To insure your faithfulness, you must remain at present under guard." Saying which, he rang a silver bell by his side, and issued a verbal order to the attendant who answered it. Immediately after, the officer of the watch entered, and Marti was placed in confinement, with orders to render him comfortable until he was sent for. His name remained a secret with the commander; and thus the night scene closed.

On the following day, one of the men-of-war that lay idly beneath the guns of Moro Castle suddenly became the scene of utmost activity, and, before noon, had weighed her anchor, and was standing out into the gulf stream. Marti, the smuggler, was on board, as her pilot; and faithfully did he guide the ship, on the discharge of his treacherous business, among the shoals and bays of the coast for nearly a month, revealing every secret haunt of the rovers, exposing their most valuable depots and well-selected rendezvous; and many a smuggling craft was taken and destroyed. The amount of money and property thus secured was very great; and Marti returned with the ship to claim his reward from the governor-general, who, well satisfied with the manner in which the rascal had fulfilled his agreement, and betrayed those comrades who were too faithful to be tempted to treachery themselves, summoned Marti before him.

"As you have faithfully performed your part of our agreement," said the governor-general, "I am now prepared to comply with the articles on my part. In this package you will find a free and unconditional pardon for all your past offenses against the laws. And here is an order on the treasury for —"

"Excellency, excuse me. The pardon I gladly receive. As to the sum of money you propose to give me, let me make you a proposition. Retain the money; and, in place of it, guarantee to me the right to fish in the neighborhood of the city, and declare the trade in fish contraband to all except my agents. This will richly repay me, and I will erect a public market of stone at my own expense, which shall be an ornament to the city, and which at the expiration of a specified number of years shall revert to the government, with all right and title to the fishery."

Tacon was pleased at the idea of a superb fish-market, which should eventually revert to the government, and also at the idea of saving the large sum of money covered by the promised reward. The singular proposition of the smuggler was duly considered and acceded to, and Marti was declared in legal form to possess for the future sole right to fish in the neighborhood of the city, or to sell the article in any form, and he at once assumed the rights that the order guaranteed to him. Having in his roving life learned all the best fishing-grounds he furnished the city bountifully with the article, and reaped yearly an immense profit, until, at the close of the period for which the monopoly was granted, he was the richest man on the island. According to the agreement, the fine market and its privilege reverted to the government at the time specified, and the monopoly has ever since been rigorously enforced.

Marti, now possessed of immense wealth, looked about him, to see in what way he could most profitably invest it to insure a handsome and sure return. The idea struck him if he could obtain the monopoly of theatricals in Havana on some such conditions as he had done that of the right to fish off its shores, he could still further increase his ill-gotten wealth. He obtained the monopoly, on condition that he should erect one of the largest and finest theatres in the world, which he did, as herein described, locating the same just outside the city walls. With the conditions of the monopoly, the writer is not conversant.

Many romantic stories are told of Marti; but the one we have here related is the only one that is authenticated.

Sophia Peabody Hawthorne

A letter from Cuba, 1834

San Marcos. La Recompenza. January 13, 1834.
My Dearest Mother,
   This is but the third letter I have written to America...
Instead of writing such numbers of epistles in the vessel as I antici-
pated, I found I could do nothing but look abroad and dream and
meditate. Every thing was so new, and glorious, and vast, that I
could not fix my mind or eyes upon a sheet of paper, seldom upon a
book, and the ocean was just as full of charm and novelty and interest
the day we anchored in the harbour of Havana as on the day we
sailed from Boston. I could not bear to leave it or our dear little
world where we had all been so happy together. Mary was indefati-
gably industrious and dispatched books and pincushions, the latter

by the dozen, besides writing a journal constantly. I read the twenti-
eth part of a book, a few stanzas of Childe Harold, studied a little
Spanish and made one pincushion! Oh yes, I marked one of the Captain's new table clothes with a T.H. which excited the admiration of
the whole ship's company. I spied a great deal with the Captain's
glass at distant ships and land whenever they were in sight. I saw
the first Palm tree wave through the glass, which gave me a strange
consciousness that I was approaching a foreign land.

Our entrance into the harbour was beautiful. Moro Castle did
not look as I thought; but it was very grand never the less. Two other vessels entered about the time we did from the United States, one
containing Mr Curson, the other Mrs Williams. We were no sooner
anchored than the government boats came out to us. The first was
rowed by 12 men in livery at one end, and under an awning at the
other sat the officers. The King's flag floated in the sea from a staff
with a strip of black drape in memory of his death. After this boat
left us, the other came up, much less stylish, to enquire about the
health of our vessels. We had hardly been there an hour before Mr
Morland and a certain Mr Bruce suddenly appeared on deck. Horace
had gone on shore in the first boat and immediately got us a permit
from the governor, like a good boy. So before we could realize we
had arrived we were sailing in a nice little green boat towards land,
with Mr Morland and Mr Bruce. We stopped at the ship Mrs Williams
came in, and took her with us. Two Spaniards rowed our boat, looking exquisitely nice and cool, dressed in white linen with worked
bosoms to their shirts.

Mr M. said that Havana was perfectly healthy. So we Sprung
upon the soil of Cuba with quite a feeling of security. Mr Bruce took
us under his arms and in a very short time we were mounting the
stone steps of Mr Cleveland's house. Mrs C. received us with open
arms, with all the warmth of her nature; but she was so dreadfully
changed in appearance that I felt really faint at seeing her. Mr Cleveland is not so changed but looks much more feeble. His suite of
rooms is in the third story and extremely lofty, unceiled, with stone
floors laid in diamonds. The drawing room is carpeted with straw;
but the hall is in a state of nature. The windows are all very wide
and high and open to the floor and lead out upon little balconies.
The custom house is on one side of the house, at the gate of which
two soldiers are perpetually on guard.

There is a very narrow peep at the bay from one window and the never ceasing song of the negroes as they raise the sugar and coffee into the ships is enough to create a slow fever. The street cries of men and women with fruits upon their heads, the squalls of children, the continuous stream of talk from groups all about, uttered in the highest key, the monotonous hammering of coopers & tinkers, the screams of macaws & parrots and all the unmusical birds that make a grand noise; the roarings and gibbering of a company of Catalans who occupy rooms under Mrs Cleveland's, almost put me beside myself.

Add to all this gales, not "from Araby the blest" which obliges you to "shut your nose," as Carlito Morrell says, and you will have some idea of the physical comfort to be found in Havana.

No wonder that Mrs Cleveland is worn out after living five years in Such a Babel without one moment of quiet. Oh, I forgot the bells! the bells! They are never Still. Tinkle, tinkle, bang, bang, squeak, squeak from morning till night and from night till morning, and at dawn a drum goes round to call the soldiers, played by a man with no ear for music, which sets every nerve on edge. The Spaniards worship noise. It is the god of theirs Idolatry, together with dirt.

Our journey from Havana apart from the wracking over the horrid roads was beautiful. We passed magnificent estates among which the marquis of Thamos was by no means the least superb. Oh such rows of palms! You have never conceived of any thing so splendid as that tree and we passed rows that were miles in length all alike, like a company of columns of white marble with a corinthian capital of green. Mr Burroughs, Carlos, a confidential servant of Dr Morrell, and Andres, who drove the horses were our escort, and we were most carefully attended.

Mr B. and Carlos were on horseback, and we stopped at almost every public place to get naranjada (orange water) & rest awhile, and at the half way house I lay down. We arrived at Mrs Morrell's at sunset, and Louisa received us very sweetly.

I soon went to bed as you may suppose & slept soundly all night! I sleep very well and have a fine appetite, and have not had a touch of cold in my head to which I am so subject at home. I ride on horseback before breakfast, nay before sunrise, and then lie down two hours, and as soon as the shadows grow long, ride again till dusk. We breakfast at 1/2 past nine, and dine at 1/2 past three, and take tea at 1/2 past eight. In the early morning coffee and oranges are at our service & at breakfast there are eggs and meat, plantains and coffee and milk, and coffee after dinner.

My head still aches a great deal, and I have not got over my weariness, but I think both will yield in due time to such a climate. Every morning there is a golden sunrise, every evening a golden sunset. The stars are of every colour of the rainbow and this January moon is the brightest of the year. It is perfectly cool excepting at midday and even then *I* am not too warm. I have on my merino dress now, which I have not taken off since I returned from my morning ride. Dr Morrell has taken my case in hand and determines to cure me. He is very interesting & Mrs Morrell is perfectly charming. The estates are beautiful. I shall describe them in some future letter. San Juan is the name of the other. Edwardo is generally my cavalier and we ride to the most enchanting places; but never off Dr M's estates which are very large. I ride upon a serron, which is a pillow with a sort of basket upon it, easy as possible, my horse Rosillo is very good. We gathered beautiful flowers this morning, and broke our fast upon oranges, which we plucked from the tree with our own hands. I have no more time the mail goes. Love to Mary N. Thine ever, ever, dearest Mother & Father,

Sophy.

William Cullen Bryant

A letter from Havana, 1849

Havana, April 10, 1849

I find that it requires a greater effort of resolution to sit down to the writing of a long letter in this soft climate, than in the country I have left. I feel a temptation to sit idly, and let the grateful wind from the sea, coming in at the broad windows, flow around me, or read, or talk, as I happen to have a book or a companion. That there is something in a tropical climate which indisposes one to vigorous exertion I can well believe, from what I experience in myself, and what I see around me. The ladies do not seem to take the least exercise, except an occasional drive on the Paseo, or public park; they never walk out, and when they are shopping, which is no less the vocation of their sex here than in other civilized countries, they never descend from their *volantes,* but the goods are brought out by the obsequious shopkeeper, and the lady makes her choice and discusses the price as she sits in her carriage.

Yet the women of Cuba show no tokens of delicate health. Freshness of color does not belong to a latitude so near the equator, but they have plump figures, placid, unwrinkled countenances, a well developed bust, and eyes, the brilliant languor of which is not the languor of illness. The girls, as well as the young men, have rather narrow shoulders, but as they advance in life, the chest, in the women particularly, seems to expand from year to year, till it attains an amplitude by no means common in our country. I fully believe that this effect, and their general health, in spite of the inaction in which they pass their lives, is owing to the free circulation of air through their apartments.

For in Cuba, the women as well as the men may be said to live in the open air. They know nothing of close rooms, in all the island, and nothing of foul air, and to this, I have no doubt, quite as much as to the mildness of the temperature, the friendly effect of its climate upon invalids from the north is to be ascribed. Their ceilings are extremely lofty, and the wide windows, extending from the top of the room to the floor and guarded by long perpendicular bars of iron, are without glass, and when closed are generally only closed with blinds which, while they break the force of the wind when it is too strong, do not exclude the air. Since I have been on the island, I may be said to have breakfasted and dined and supped and slept in the open air, in an atmosphere which is never in repose except for a short time in the morning after sunrise. At other times a breeze is always stirring, in the daytime bringing in the air from the ocean, and at night drawing it out again to the sea.

In walking through the streets of the towns in Cuba, I have been entertained by the glimpses I had through the ample windows, of what was going on in the parlors. Sometimes a curtain hanging before them allowed me only a sight of the small hands which clasped the bars of the grate, and the dusky faces and dark eyes peeping into the street and scanning the passers by. At other times, the whole room was seen, with its furniture, and its female forms sitting in languid postures, courting the breeze as it entered from without. In the evening, as I passed along the narrow sidewalk of the narrow streets, I have been startled at finding myself almost in the midst of a merry party gathered about the window of a brilliantly lighted room, and chattering the soft Spanish of the island in voices that sounded strangely near to me. I have spoken of their languid postures: they love to recline on sofas; their houses are filled with rocking chairs imported from the United States; they are fond of sitting in chairs tilted against the wall, as we sometimes do at home. Indeed they go beyond us in this respect; for in Cuba they have invented a kind of chair which, by lowering the back and raising the knees, places the sitter precisely in the posture he would take if he sat in a chair leaning backward against a wall. It is a luxurious attitude, I must own, and I do not wonder that it is a favorite with lazy people, for it relieves one of all the trouble of keeping the body upright.

It is the women who form the large majority of the worshippers in the churches. I landed here in Passion Week, and the next day was Holy Thursday, when not a vehicle on wheels of any sort is allowed to be seen in the streets; and the ladies, contrary to their custom during the rest of the year, are obliged to resort to the churches on foot. Negro servants of both sexes were seen passing to and fro, carrying mats on which their mistresses were to kneel in the morning service. All the white female population, young and old, were dressed in black, with black lace veils. In the afternoon, three wooden or waxen images of the size of life, representing Christ in the different stages of his passion, were placed in the spacious Church of St. Catharine, which was so thronged that I found it difficult to enter. Near the door was a figure of the Saviour sinking under the weight of his cross, and the worshippers were kneeling to kiss his feet. Aged negro men and women, half-naked negro children, ladies richly attired, little girls in Parisian dresses, with lustrous black eyes and a profusion of ringlets, cast themselves down before the image, and pressed their lips to its feet in a passion of devotion. Mothers led up their little ones, and showed them how to perform this act of adoration. I saw matrons and young women rise from it with their eyes red with tears.

The next day, which was Good Friday, about twilight, a long procession came trailing slowly through the streets under my window, bearing an image of the dead Christ, lying upon a cloth of gold. It was accompanied by a body of soldiery, holding their muskets reversed, and a band playing plaintive tunes; the crowd uncovered their heads as it passed. On Saturday morning, at ten o'clock, the solemnities of holy week were over; the bells rang a merry peal; hundreds of *volantes* and drays which had stood ready harnessed, rushed into the streets; the city became suddenly noisy with the rattle of wheels and the tramp of horses; the shops, which had been shut for the last two days, were opened; and the ladies, in white or light-colored muslins, were proceeding in their *volantes* to purchase at the shops their costumes for the Easter festivities.

I passed the evening on the *Plaza de Armas,* a public square in front of the governor's house, planted with palms and other trees, paved with broad flags, and bordered with a row of benches. It was crowded with people in their best dresses, the ladies mostly in white, and without bonnets, for the bonnet in this country is only worn while travelling. Chairs had been placed for them in a double row around the edge of the square, and a row of *volantes* surrounded the square, in each of which sat two or more ladies, the ample folds of their muslin dresses flowing out on each side over the steps of the carriage. The governor's band played various airs, martial and civic, with great beauty of execution. The music continued for two hours, and the throng, with only occasional intervals of conversation, seemed to give themselves up wholly to the enjoyment of listening to it.

It was a bright moonlight night, so bright that one might almost see to read, and the temperature the finest I can conceive, a gentle breeze rustling among the palms overhead. I was surprised at seeing around me so many fair brows and snowy necks. It is the moonlight, said I to myself or perhaps it is the effect of the white dresses, for the complexions of these ladies seem to differ several shades from those which I saw yesterday at the churches. A female acquaintance has since given me another solution of the matter.

"The reason," she said, "of the difference you perceived is this, that during the ceremonies of holy week they take off the *cascarilla* from their faces, and appear in their natural complexions."

I asked the meaning of the word *cascarilla,* which I did not remember to have heard before.

"It is the favorite cosmetic of the island, and is made of egg-shells finely pulverized. They often fairly plaster their faces with it. I have seen a dark-skinned lady as white almost as marble at a ball. They will sometimes, at a morning call or an evening party, withdraw to repair the *cascarilla* on their faces."

I do not vouch for this tale, but tell it "as it was told to me." Perhaps, after all, it was the moonlight which had produced this transformation, though I had noticed something of the same improvement of complexion just before sunset, on the Paseo Isabel, a public park without the city walls, planted with rows of trees, where, every afternoon, the gentry of Havana drive backward and forward in their *volantes*, with each a glittering harness, and a livened negro bestriding, in large jack-boots, the single horse which draws the vehicle.

I had also the same afternoon visited the receptacle into which the population of the city are swept when the game of life is played out — the Camp Santo, as it is called, or public cemetery of Havana. Going out of the city at the gate nearest the sea, I passed through a street of the wretchedest houses I had seen; the ocean was roaring at my right on the coral rocks which form the coast. The dingy habitations were soon left behind, and I saw the waves, pushed forward by a fresh wind, flinging their spray almost into the road; I next entered a short avenue of trees, and in a few minutes the *volante* stopped at the gate of the cemetery. In a little inclosure before the entrance, a few starveling flowers of Europe were cultivated, but the wild plants of the country flourished luxuriantly on the rich soil within. A thick wall surrounded the cemetery, in which were rows of openings for coffins, one above the other, where the more opulent of the dead were entombed. The coffin is thrust in endwise, and the opening closed with a marble slab bearing an inscription.

Most of these niches were already occupied, but in the earth below, by far the greater part of those who die at Havana, are buried without a monument or a grave which they are allowed to hold a longer time than is necessary for their bodies to be consumed in the quicklime which is thrown upon them. Every day fresh trenches are dug into which their bodies are thrown, generally without coffins. Two of these, one near each wall of the cemetery, were waiting for the funerals. I saw where the spade had divided the bones of those who were buried there last, and thrown up the broken fragments, mingled with masses of lime, locks of hair, and bits of clothing. Without the walls was a receptacle in which the skulls and other larger bones, dark with the mould of the grave, were heaped.

Two or three persons were walking about the cemetery when we first entered, but it was now at length the cool of the day, and the funerals began to arrive. They brought in first a rude black coffin, broadest at the extremity which contained the head, and placing it at the end of one of the trenches, hurriedly produced a hammer and nails to fasten the lid before letting it down, when it was found that the box was too shallow at the narrower extremity. The lid was removed for a moment and showed the figure of an old man in a threadbare black coat, white pantaloons, and boots. The negroes who bore it beat out the bottom with the hammer, so as to allow the lid to be fastened over the feet. It was then nailed down firmly with coarse nails, the coffin was swung into the trench, and the earth shovelled upon it. A middle-aged man, who seemed to be some relative of the dead, led up a little boy close to the grave and watched the process of filling it. They spoke to each other and smiled, stood till the pit was filled to the surface, and the bearers had departed, and then retired in their turn. This was one the more respectable class of funerals. Commonly the dead are piled without coffins, one above the other, in the trenches.

The funerals now multiplied. The corpse of a little child was brought in, uncoffined; and another, a young man who, I was told, had cut his throat for love, was borne towards one of the niches in the wall. I heard loud voices, which seemed to proceed from the eastern side of the cemetery, and which, I thought at first, might be the recitation of a funeral service; but no funeral service is said at these graves; and after a time, I perceived that they came from the windows of a long building which overlooked one side of the burial ground. It was a mad-house. The inmates, exasperated at the spectacle before them, gesticulating from the windows — the women screaming and the men shouting, but no attention was paid to their uproar. A lady, however, a stranger to the island, who visited the Campo Santo that afternoon, was so affected by the sights and sounds of the place, that she was borne out weeping and almost in convulsions. As we left the place, we found a crowd of *volantes* about the gate; a pompous bier, with rich black hangings, drew up; a little beyond, we met one of another kind — a long box, with glass sides and ends, in which lay the corpse of a woman, dressed in white, with a black veil thrown over the face.

The next day the festivities, which were to indemnify the people for the austerities of Lent and of Passion Week, began. The cock-pits were opened during the day, and masked balls were given in the evening at the theatres. You know, probably, that cock-fighting is the principal diversion of the island, having entirely supplanted the national spectacle of bull-baiting. Cuba, in fact, seemed to me a great poultry-yard. I heard the crowing of cocks in all quarters, for the game-cock is the noisiest and most beautiful of birds, and is perpetually uttering his notes of defiance. In the villages I saw the veterans of the pit, a strong-legged race, with their combs cropped smooth to the head, the feathers plucked from every part of the body except their wings, and the tail docked like that of a coach horse, picking up their food in the lanes among the chickens. One old cripple I remember to have seen in the little town of Guines, stiff with wounds received in combat, who had probably got a furlough for life, and who, while limping among his female companions, maintained a sort of strut in his gait, and now and then stopped to crow defiance to the world. The peasants breed game-cocks and bring them to market; amateurs in the town train them for their private amusement. Dealers in game-cocks are as common as horse-jockies with us, and every village has its cock-pit.

I went on Monday to the *Valla de Gallos* situated in that part of Havana which lies without walls. Here, in a spacious inclosure, were two amphitheatres of benches, roofed, but without walls, with a circular area in the midst. Each was crowded with people, who were looking at a cockfight, and half of whom seemed vociferating with all their might. I mounted one of the outer benches, and saw one of the birds laid dead by the other in a few minutes. Then was heard the chink of gold and silver pieces, as the betters stepped into the area and paid their wagers; the slain bird was carried out and thrown on the ground, and the victor, taken into the hands of his owner, crowed loudly in celebration of his victory. Two other birds were brought in, and the cries of those who offered wagers were heard on all sides. They ceased at last, and the cocks were put down to begin the combat. They fought warily at first, but at length began to strike in earnest, the blood flowed, and the bystanders were heard to vociferate, *"Ahi están peleando!"* —*"Mata! Mata! Mata!"* (*"Now they are fighting!"* — *"Kill! kill! kill!"*) gesticulating at the same time with great violence, and new wagers were laid as the interest of the combat increased. In 10 minutes one of the birds was dispatched, for the combat never ends till one of them has his death-wound.

In the meantime several other combats had begun in smaller pits, which lay within the same inclosure, but were not surrounded with circles of benches. I looked upon the throng engaged in this brutal sport, with eager gestures and loud cries, and could not help thinking how soon this noisy crowd would lie in heaps in the pits of the Campo Santo.

In the evening was a masked ball in the Tacon Theatre, a spacious building, one of the largest of its kind in the world. The pit, floored over, with the whole depth of the stage open to the back wall of the edifice, furnished a ballroom of immense size. People in grotesque masks, in hoods or fancy dresses, were mingled with a throng clad in the ordinary costume, and Spanish dances were performed to the music of a numerous band. A well-dressed crowd filled the first and second tier of boxes. The Creole smokes everywhere, and seemed astonished when the soldier who stood at the door ordered him to throw away his lighted segar before entering. Once upon the floor, however, he lighted another segar in defiance of the prohibition.

The Spanish dances, with their graceful movements, resembling the undulations of the sea in its gentlest moods, are nowhere more gracefully performed than in Cuba by the young women born on the island. I could not help thinking, however, as I looked on that gay crowd, on the quaint maskers, and the dancers whose flexible limbs seemed swayed to and fro by the breath of the music, that all this was soon to end at the Campo Santo, and I asked myself how many of all this crowd would be huddled uncoffined, when their sports were over, into the foul trenches of the public cemetery.

Richard Henry Dana Jr.

Havana, 1859

We coast the northern shore of Cuba, from Matanzas westward. There is no waste of sand and low flats, as in most of our southern states; but the fertile, undulating land comes to the sea, and rises into high hills as it recedes. "There is the Morro! and right ahead!" "Why, there is the city too! Is the city on the sea? We thought it was on a harbor or bay." There, indeed, is the Morro, a stately hill of tawny rock, rising perpendicularly from the sea, and jutting into it, with walls and parapets and towers on its top, and flags and signals flying, and the tall lighthouse just in front of its outer wall. It is not very high, yet commands the sea about it. And there is the city, on the seacoast, indeed — the houses running down to the coral edge of the ocean. Where is the harbor, and where the shipping? Ah, there they are! We open an entrance, narrow and deep, between the beetling Morro and the Punta; and through the entrance, we see the spreading harbor and the innumerable masts. But the darkness is gathering, the sunset gun has been fired, we can just catch the dying notes of trumpets from the fortifications, and the Morro Lighthouse throws its gleam over the still sea. The little lights emerge and twinkle from the city. We are too late to enter the port, and slowly and reluctantly the ship turns her head off to seaward. The engine breathes heavily, and throws its one arm leisurely up and down; we rise and fall on the moonlit sea; the stars are near to us, or we are raised nearer to them; the Southern Cross is just above the horizon; and all night long, two streams of light lie upon the water, one of gold from the Morro, and one of silver from the moon. It is enchantment. Who can regret our delay, or wish to exchange this scene for the common, close anchorage of a harbor?

We are to go in at sunrise, and few, if any, are the passengers that are not on deck at the first glow of dawn. Before us lie the novel and exciting objects of the night before. The Steep Morro, with its tall sentinel lighthouse, and its towers and signal staffs and teeth of guns, is coming out into clear daylight; the red and yellow striped flag of Spain — blood and gold — floats over it. Point after point in the city becomes visible; the blue and white and yellow houses, with their roofs of dull red tiles, the quaint old Cathedral towers, and the almost endless lines of fortifications. The masts of the immense shipping rise over the headland, the signal for leave to enter is run up, and we steer in under full head, the morning gun thundering from the Morro, the trumpets braying and drums beating from all the fortifications, the Morro, the Punta, the long Cabana, the Casa Blanca and the city walls, while the broad sun is fast rising over this magnificent spectacle.

What a world of shipping! The masts make a belt of dense forest along the edge of the city, all the ships lying head in to the street, like horses at their mangers; while the vessels at anchor nearly choke up the passage ways to the deeper bays beyond. There are the red and yellow stripes of decayed Spain; the blue, white and red — blood to the fingers' end — of La Grande Nation; the Union crosses of the Royal Commonwealth; the stars and stripes of the Great Republic, and a few flags of Holland and Portugal, of the states of northern Italy, of Brazil, and of the republics of the Spanish Maine. We thread our slow and careful way among these, pass under the broadside of a ship-of-the-line, and under the stern of a screw frigate, both bearing the Spanish flag, and cast our anchor in the Regla Bay, by the side of the steamer *Karnac,* which sailed from New York a few days before us. Instantly we are besieged by boats, some loaded with oranges and bananas, and others coming for passengers and their luggage, all with awnings spread over their sterns, rowed by sallow, attenuated men, in blue and white checks and straw hats, with here and there the familiar lips and teeth, and vacant, easily-pleased face of the Negro. Among these boats comes one, from the stern of which floats the red and yellow flag with the crown in its field, and under whose awning reclines a man in a full suit of white linen, with straw hat and red cockade and a cigar. This is the Health Officer. Until he is satisfied, no one can come on board, or leave the vessel. Capt. Bullock salutes, steps down the ladder to the boat, hands his papers, reports all well — and we are pronounced safe. Then comes another boat of similar style, another man reclining under the awning with a cigar, who comes on board, is closeted with the purser, compares the passenger list with the passports, and we are declared fully passed, and general leave is given to land with our luggage at the custom-house wharf.

Now comes the war of cries and gestures and grimaces among the boatmen, in their struggle for passengers, increased manifold by the fact that there is but little language in common between the parties to the bargains, and by the boatmen being required to remain in their boats. How thin these boatmen look! You cannot get it out of your mind that they must all have had the yellow fever last summer, and are not yet fully recovered. Not only their faces, but their hands and arms and legs are thin, and their low-quartered slippers only half cover their thin yellow feet.

In the hurry, I have to hunt after the passengers I am to take leave of who go on to New Orleans: — Mr. and Mrs. Benchley, on their way to their intended new home in western Texas, my two sea captains, and the little son of my friend, who is the guest, on this voyage, of our common friend the captain, and after all, I miss the hearty handshake of Bullock and Rodgers. Seated under an awning, in the stern of a boat, with my trunk and carpet-bag and an unseasonable bundle of Arctic overcoat and fur cap in the bow, I am pulled by a man with an oar in each hand and a cigar in mouth, to the custom-house pier. Here is a busy scene of trunks, carpet-bags, and bundles; and up and down the pier marches a military grandee of about the rank of a sergeant or sub-lieutenant, with a preposterous strut, so out of keeping with the depressed military character of his country, and not possible to be appreciated without seeing it. If he would give that strut on the boards, in New York, he would draw full houses nightly.

Our passports are kept, and we receive a license to remain and travel in the island, good for three months only, for which a large fee is paid. These officers of the customs are civil and reasonably rapid; and in a short time my luggage is on a dray driven by a Negro, and I am in a *volante*, managed by a Negro postilion, and am driving through the narrow streets of this surprising city.

The streets are so narrow and the houses built so close upon them, that they seem to be rather spaces between the walls of houses than highways for travel. It appears impossible that two vehicles should pass abreast; yet they do so. There are constant blockings of the way. In some places awnings are stretched over the entire street, from house to house, and we are riding under a long tent. What strange vehicles these *volantes* are! — A pair of very long, limber shafts, at one end of which is a pair of huge wheels, and the other end a horse with his tail braided and brought forward and tied to the saddle, an open chaise body resting on the shafts, about one third of the way from the axle to the horse; and on the horse is a Negro, in large postilion boots, long spurs, and a bright jacket. It is an easy vehicle to ride in; but it must be a sore burden to the beast. Here and there we pass a private *volante*, distinguished by rich silver mountings and postilions in livery. Some have two horses, and with the silver and the livery and the long dangling traces and a look of superfluity, have rather an air of high life. In most, a gentleman is reclining, cigar in mouth; while in others, is a great puff of blue or pink muslin or cambric, extending over the sides to the shafts, topped off by a fan, with signs of a face behind it. "Calle de los Oficios," "Calle del Obispo," "Calle de San Ignacio," "Calle de Mercaderes," are on the little corner boards. Every little shop and every big shop has its title; but nowhere does the name of a keeper appear. Almost every shop advertises "por mayor y menor," wholesale and retail. What a Gil Blas-Don Quixote feeling the names of "posada," "tienda," and "cantina" give you!

There are no women walking in the streets, except Negresses.

Those suits of seersucker, with straw hats and red cockades, are soldiers. It is a sensible dress for the climate. Every third man, perhaps more, and not a few women, are smoking cigars or cigarritos. Here are things moving along, looking like cocks of new mown grass, under way. But presently you see the head of a horse or mule peering out from under the mass, and a tail is visible at the other end, and feet are picking their slow way over the stones. These are the carriers of green fodder, the fresh cut stalks and blades of corn; and my chance companion in the carriage, a fellow passenger by the "Cahawba," a Frenchman, who has been here before, tells me that they supply all the horses and mules in the city with their daily feed, as no hay is used. There are also mules, asses, and horses with bananas, plantains, oranges, and other fruits in panniers reaching almost to the ground.

Here is the Plaza de Armas, with its garden of rich, fragrant flowers in full bloom, in front of the governor's Palace. At the corner is the chapel erected over the spot where, under the auspices of Columbus, mass was first celebrated on the island. We are driven past a gloomy convent, past innumerable shops, past drinking places, billiard rooms, and the thick, dead walls of houses, with large windows, grated like dungeons, and large gates, showing glimpses of interior courtyards, sometimes with trees and flowers. But horses and carriages and gentlemen and ladies and slaves, all seem to use the same entrance. The windows come to the ground, and, being flush with the street, and mostly without glass, nothing but the grating prevents a stranger from walking into the rooms. And there the ladies and children sit sewing, or lounging, or playing…

The men wear black dress coats, long pantaloons, black cravats, and many of them even submit, in this hot sun, to black French hats…

We drove through the Puerta de Monserrate, a heavy gateway of the prevailing yellow or tawny color, where soldiers are on guard, across the moat, out upon the "Paseo de Isabel Segunda," and are now *extramuros*, without the walls. The Paseo is a grand avenue running across the city from sea to bay, with two carriage-drives abreast, and two malls for foot passengers, and all lined with trees in full foliage. Here you catch a glimpse of the Morro, and there of the Presidio. This is the Teatro de Tacón; and, in front of this line of tall houses, in contrast with the almost uniform one-story buildings of the city, the *volante* stops. This is Le Grand's hotel.

To a person unaccustomed to the tropics or the south of Europe, I know of nothing more discouraging than the arrival at the inn or hotel. It is nobody's business to attend to you. The landlord is strangely indifferent, and if there is a way to get a thing done, you have not learned it, and there is no one to teach you. Le Grand is a Frenchman. His house is a restaurant, with rooms for lodgers. The restaurant is paramount. The lodging is secondary, and is left to servants. Monsieur does not condescend to show a room, even to families; and the servants, who are whites, but mere lads, have all the interior in their charge, and there are no women employed about the chambers. Antonio, a swarthy Spanish lad, in shirt sleeves, looking very much as if he never washed, has my part of the house in charge, and shows me my room. It has but one window, a door opening upon the veranda, and a brick floor, and is very bare of furniture, and the furniture has long ceased to be strong. A small stand barely holds up a basin and ewer which have not been washed since Antonio was washed, and the bedstead, covered by a canvas sacking, without mattress or bed, looks as if it would hardly bear the weight of a man. It is plain there is a good deal to be learned here. Antonio is communicative, on a suggestion of several days' stay and good pay. Things which we cannot do without, we must go out of the house to find, and those which we can do without, we must dispense with. This is odd, and strange, but not uninteresting, and affords scope for contrivance and the exercise of influence and other administrative powers. The Grand Seigneur does not mean to be troubled with anything; so there are no bells, and no office, and no clerks. He is the only source, and if he is approached, he shrugs his shoulders and gives you to understand that you have your chambers for your money and must look to the servants. Antonio starts off on an expedition for a pitcher of water and a towel, with a faint hope of two towels; for each demand involves an expedition to remote parts of the house. Then Antonio has so many rooms dependent on him that every door is a Scylla, and every window a Charybdis, as he passes. A shrill, female voice, from the next room but one, calls "Antonio! Antonio!" and that starts the parrot in the courtyard, who cries "Antonio! Antonio!" for several minutes. A deep, bass voice mutters "Antonio!" in a more confidential tone; and last of all, an unmistakably Northern voice attempts it, but ends in something between Antonio and Anthony. He is gone a good while, and has evidently had several episodes to his journey. But he is a good-natured fellow, speaks a little French, very little English, and seems anxious to do his best.

I see the faces of my New York fellow-passengers from the west gallery, and we come together and throw our acquisitions of information into a common stock, and help one another. Mr. Miller's servant, who has been here before, says there are baths and other conveniences round the corner of the street; and, sending our bundles of thin clothes there, we take advantage of the baths, with comfort. To be sure, we must go through a billiard-room, where the Creoles are playing at the tables, and the cockroaches playing under them, and through a drinking-room, and a bowling-alley; but the baths are built in the open yard, protected by blinds, well ventilated, and well supplied with water and toilet apparatus.

With the comfort of a bath, and clothed in linen, with straw hats, we walk back to Le Grand's, and enter the restaurant, for breakfast — the breakfast of the country, at ten o'clock. Here is a scene so pretty as quite to make up for the defects of the chambers. The restaurant with cool marble floor, walls 24 feet high, open rafters painted blue, great windows open to the floor and looking into the Paseo, and the floor nearly on a level with the street, a light breeze fanning the thin curtains, the little tables, for two or four, with clean, white cloths, each with its pyramid of great red oranges and its fragrant bouquet — the gentlemen in white pantaloons and jackets and white stockings, and the ladies in fly-away muslins, and hair in the sweet neglect of the morning toilet, taking their leisurely breakfasts of fruit and claret, and omelette and Spanish mixed dishes (ollas), and café noir. How airy and ethereal it seems! They are birds, not substantial men and women. They eat ambrosia and drink nectar. It must be that they fly, and live in nests, in the tamarind trees. Who can eat a hot, greasy breakfast of cakes and gravied meats, and in a close room, after this?

I can truly say that I ate, this morning, my first orange; for I had never before eaten one newly gathered, which had ripened in the sun, hanging on the tree. We call for the usual breakfast, leaving the selection to the waiter; and he brings us fruits, claret, omelette, fish fresh from the sea, rice excellently cooked, fried plantains, a mixed dish of meat and vegetables (olla), and coffee. The fish, I do not remember its name, is boiled, and has the colors of the rainbow, as it lies on the plate. Havana is a good fishmarket; for it is as open to the ocean as Nahant, or the beach at Newport; its streets running to the blue sea, outside the harbor, so that a man may almost throw his line from the curbstone into the Gulf Stream.

After breakfast, I take a *volante* and ride into the town, to deliver my letters. Three merchants whom I call upon have palaces for their business. The entrances are wide, the staircases almost as stately as that of Stafford House, the floors of marble, the panels of porcelain tiles, the rails of iron, and the rooms over 20 feet high, with open rafters, the doors and windows colossal, the furniture rich and heavy; and there sits the merchant or banker, in white pantaloons and thin shoes and loose white coat and narrow necktie, smoking a succession of cigars, surrounded by tropical luxuries and tropical protections. In the lower story of one of these buildings is an exposition of silks, cotton, and linens, in a room so large that it looked like a part of the Great Exhibition in Hyde Park. At one of these counting-palaces, I met Mr. Theodore Parker and Dr. S. G. Howe, of Boston, who preceded me, in the *Karnac*. Mr. Parker is here for his health, which has caused anxiety to his friends lest his weakened frame should no longer support the strong intellectual machinery as before. He finds Havana too hot, and will leave for Santa Cruz by the first opportunity…

The Bishop of Havana has been in delicate health, and is out of town, at Jesus del Monte, and Miss M. is not at home, and the Senoras F. — I failed to see this morning; but I found a Boston young lady, whose friends were desirous I should see her, and who was glad enough to meet one so lately from her home…

In the latter part of the afternoon, from three o'clock, our parties are taking dinner at Le Grand's. The little tables are again full, with a fair complement of ladies. The afternoon breeze is so strong that the draught of air, though it is hot air, is to be avoided. The passers-by almost put their faces into the room, and the women and children of the poorer order look wistfully in upon the luxurious guests, the colored glasses, the red wines, and the golden fruits. The Opera troupe is here, both the singers and the ballet; and we have… the benefit of a rehearsal, at nearly all hours of the day, of operas that the Habaneros are to rave over at night.

I yield to no one in my admiration of the Spanish as a spoken language, whether in its rich, sonorous, musical, and lofty style, in the mouth of a man who knows its uses, or in the soft, indolent, languid tones of a woman, broken by an occasional birdlike trill —

"With wanton heed, and giddy cunning,
The melting voice through mazes running"

— but I do not like it as spoken by the common people of Cuba, in the streets. Their voices and intonations are thin and eager, very rapid, too much in the lips, and, withal, giving an impression of the passionate and the childish combined; and it strikes me that the tendency here is to enfeeble the language, and take from it the openness of the vowels and the strength of the harder consonants. This is the criticism of a few hours' observation, and may not be just; but I have heard the same from persons who have been longer acquainted with it. Among the well-educated Cubans, the standard of Castilian is said to be kept high, and there is a good deal of ambition to reach it.

After dinner, walked along the Paseo de Isabel Segunda to see the pleasure-driving, which begins at about five o'clock, and lasts until dark. The most common carriage is the *volante*, but there are some carriages in the English style, with servants in livery on the box. I have taken a fancy for the strange-looking two-horse *volante*. The postilion, the long, dangling traces, the superfluousness of a horse to be ridden by the man that guides the other, and the prodigality of silver, give the whole a look of style that eclipses the neat appropriate English equipage. The ladies ride in full dress, décolletées, without hats. The servants on the carriages are not all Negroes. Many of the drivers are white. The drives are along the Paseo de Isabel, across the Campo del Marte, and then along the Paseo de Tacón, a beautiful double avenue, lined with trees, which leads two or three miles, in a straight line, into the country.

At eight o'clock, drove to the Plaza de Armas, a square in front of the governor's house, to hear the Retreta, at which a military band plays for an hour every evening. There is a clear moon above, and a blue field of glittering stars; the air is pure and balmy; the band of 50 or 60 instruments discourses most eloquent music under the shade of palm trees and mangoes; the walks are filled with promenaders, and the streets around the square lined with carriages, in which the ladies recline, and receive the salutations and visits of the gentlemen. Very few ladies walk in the square, and those probably are strangers. It is against the etiquette for ladies to walk in public in Havana.

I walk leisurely home, in order to see Havana by night. The evening is the busiest season for the shops. Much of the business of shopping is done after gas lighting. *Volantes* and coaches are driving to and fro, and stopping at the shop doors, and attendants take their goods to the doors of the carriages. The watchmen stand at the corners of the streets, each carrying a long pike and a lantern. Billiard-rooms and cafés are filled, and all who can walk for pleasure will walk now. This is also the principal time for paying visits.

There is one strange custom observed here in all the houses. In the chief room, rows of chairs are placed, facing each other, three or four or five in each line, and always running at right angles with the street wall of the house. As you pass along the street, you look up this row of chairs. In these, the family and the visitors take their seats, in formal order. As the windows are open, deep, and large, with wide gratings and no glass, one has the inspection of the interior arrangement of all the front parlors of Havana, and can see what every lady wears, and who is visiting her.

★

If mosquito nets were invented for the purpose of shutting mosquitoes in with you, they answer their purpose very well. The beds have no mattresses, and you lie on the hard sacking. This favors coolness and neatness. I should fear a mattress, in the economy of our hotel, at least. Where there is nothing but an iron frame, canvas stretched over it, and sheets and a blanket, you may know what you are dealing with.

The clocks of the churches and castles strike the quarter hours, and at each stroke the watchmen blow a kind of boatswain's whistle, and cry the time and the state of the weather, which, from their name (*serenos*), should be always pleasant.

I have been advised to close the shutters at night, whatever the heat, as the change of air that often takes place before dawn is injurious; and I notice that many of the bedrooms in the hotel are closed, both doors and shutters, at night. This is too much for my endurance, and I venture to leave the air to its course, not being in the draught…

There are streaks of a clear dawn; it is nearly six o'clock, the cocks are crowing, and the drums and trumpets sounding. We have been told of sea-baths, cut in the rock, near the Punta, at the foot of our Paseo. I walk down, under the trees, toward the Presidio. What is this clanking sound? Can it be cavalry, marching on foot, their sabres rattling on the pavement? No, it comes from that crowd of poor-looking creatures that are forming in files in front of the Presidio. It is the chain-gang! Poor wretches! I come nearer to them, and wait until they are formed and numbered and marched off. Each man has an iron band riveted round his ankle, and another round his waist, and the chain is fastened, one end into each of these bands, and dangles between them, clanking with every movement. This leaves the wearers free to use their arms, and, indeed, their whole body, it being only a weight and a badge and a note for discovery, from which they cannot rid themselves. It is kept on them day and night, working, eating, or sleeping. In some cases, two are chained together. They have passed their night in the Presidio (the great prison and garrison), and are marshalled for their day's toil in the public streets and on the public works, in the heat of the sun. They look thoroughly wretched. Can any of these be political offenders? It is said that Carlists, from Old Spain, worked in this gang. Sentence to the chain-gang in summer, in the case of a foreigner, must be nearly certain death.

Farther on, between the Presidio and the Punta, the soldiers are drilling; and the drummers and trumpeters are practising on the rampart of the city walls.

A little to the left, in the Calzada de San Lázaro, are the Baños de Mar. These are boxes, each about 12 feet square and six or eight feet deep, cut directly into the rock which here forms the sea-line, with steps of rock, and each box having a couple of portholes through which the waves of this tideless shore wash in and out. This arrangement is necessary, as sharks are so abundant that bathing in the open sea is dangerous. The pure rock, and the flow and reflow, make these bathing-boxes very agreeable, and the water, which is that of the Gulf Stream, is at a temperature of 72 degrees. The baths are roofed over, and partially screened on the inside, but open for a view out, on the side towards the sea; and as you bathe, you see the big ships floating up the Gulf Stream, that great highway of the Equinoctial world. The water stands at depths of from three to five feet in the baths; and they are large enough for short swimming. The bottom is white with sand and shells. These baths are made at the public expense, and are free. Some are marked for women, some for men, and some "por la gente de color." A little further down the Calzada is another set of baths, and further out in the suburbs, opposite the Beneficencia, are still others.

After bath, took two or three fresh oranges, and a cup of coffee, without milk; for the little milk one uses with coffee must not be taken with fruit here, even in winter.

To the Cathedral, at eight o'clock, to hear mass. The Cathedral, in its exterior, is a plain and quaint old structure, with a tower at each angle of the front; but within, it is sumptuous. There is a floor of variegated marble, obstructed by no seats or screens, tall pillars and rich frescoed walls, and delicate masonry of various colored stone, the prevailing tint being yellow, and a high altar of porphyry. There is a look of the great days of Old Spain about it; and you think that knights and nobles worshipped here and enriched it from their spoils and conquests. Every new eye turns first to the place within the choir, under that alto-relief, behind that short inscription, where, in the wall of the chancel, rest the remains of Christopher Columbus. Borne from Valladolid to Seville, from Seville to San Domingo, and from San Domingo to Havana, they at last rest here, by the altar side, in the emporium of the Spanish Islands. "What is man that thou art mindful of him!" truly and humbly says the Psalmist; but what is man, indeed, if his fellow men are not mindful of such a man as this! The creator of a hemisphere! It is not often we feel that monuments are surely deserved, in their degree and to the extent of their utterance. But when, in the New World, on an island of that group which he gave to civilized man, you stand before this simple monumental slab, and know that all of him that man can gather up lies behind it, so overpowering is the sense of the greatness of his deeds, that you feel relieved that no attempt has been made to measure it by any work of man's hands...

The priests in the chancel are numerous, perhaps 20 or more. The service is chanted with no aid of instruments, except once the accompaniment of a small and rather disordered organ, and chanted in very loud and often harsh and blatant tones, which reverberate from the marble walls, with a tiresome monotony of cadence. There is a degree of ceremony in the placing, replacing, and carrying to and fro of candles and crucifixes, and swinging of censers, which the Roman service as practised in the United States does not give...

★

Breakfast, and again the cool marble floor, white-robed tables, the fruits and flowers, and curtains gently swaying, and women in morning toilets. Besides the openness to view, these rooms are strangely open to ingress. Lottery-ticket vendors go the rounds of the tables at every meal, and so do the girls with tambourines for alms for the music in the street...

Spent the morning, from eleven o'clock to dinner-time, in my room, writing and reading... The rooms all open into the courtyard, and the doors and windows, if open at all, are open to the view of all passers-by. As there are no bells, every call is made from the veranda rail, down into the courtyard, and repeated until the servant answers, or the caller gives up in despair. Antonio has a compeer and rival in Domingo, and the sharp voice of the woman in the next room but one, who proves to be a subordinate of the opera troupe, is calling out, "Do-meen-go! Do-meen-go!" and the rogue is in full sight from our side, making significant faces, until she changes her tune to "Antonio! Antonio! Adónde está Domingo?" But as she speaks very little Spanish, and Antonio very little French, it is not difficult for him to get up a misapprehension, especially at the distance of two stories; and she is obliged to subside for a while, and her place is supplied by the parrot. She is usually unsuccessful, being either unreasonable, or bad pay. The opera troupe are rehearsing in the second flight, with doors and windows open. And throughout the hot middle day, we hear the singing, the piano, the parrot, and the calls and parleys with the servants below. But we can see the illimitable sea from the end of the piazza, blue as indigo; and the strange city is lying under our eye, with its strange blue and white and yellow houses, with their roofs of dull red tiles, its strange tropical shade-trees, and its strange vehicles and motley population, and the clanging of its bells, and the high-pitched cries of the vendors in its streets.

Going down stairs at about eleven o'clock, I find a table set in the front hall, at the foot of the great staircase, and there, in full view of all who come or go, the landlord and his entire establishment, except the slaves and coolies, are at breakfast. This is done every day. At the café round the corner, the family with their white, hired servants breakfast and dine in the hall, through which all the customers of the place must go to the baths, the billiard-rooms, and the bowling-alleys. Fancy the manager of the Astor or Revere, spreading a table for breakfast and dinner in the great entry between the office and the front door, for himself and family and servants...!

After dinner drove out to the Jesus del Monte, to deliver my letter of introduction to the Bishop. The drive, by way of the Calzada de Jesus del Monte, takes one through a wretched portion, I hope the most wretched portion, of Havana, by long lines of one-story wood and mud hovels, hardly habitable even for Negroes, and interspersed with an abundance of drinking shops. The horses, mules, asses, chickens, children, and grown people use the same door; and the back yards disclose heaps of rubbish. The looks of the men, the horses tied to the door-posts, the mules with their panniers of fruits and leaves reaching to the ground, all speak of Gil Blas, and of what we have read of humble life in Spain. The little Negro children go stark naked, as innocent of clothing as the puppies. But this is so all over the city. In the front hall of Le Grand's, this morning, a lady, standing in a full dress of spotless white, held by the hand a naked little Negro boy, of two or three years old, nestling in black relief against the folds of her dress.

Now we rise to the higher grounds of Jesus del Monte. The houses improve in character. They are still of one story, but high and of stone, with marble floors and tiled roofs, with courtyards of grass and trees, and through the gratings of the wide, long, open windows, I see the decent furniture, the double, formal row of chairs, prints on the walls, and well-dressed women maneuvering their fans.

As a carriage with a pair of cream-colored horses passed, having two men within, in the dress of ecclesiastics, my driver pulled up and said that was the Bishop's carriage, and that he was going out for an evening drive. Still, I must go on; and we drive to his house. As you go up the hill, a glorious view lies upon the left. Havana, both city and suburbs, the Morro with its batteries and lighthouse, the ridge of fortifications called the Cabana and Casa Blanca, the Castle of Atares, near at hand, a perfect truncated cone, fortified at the top — the higher and most distant Castle of Principe...

The regular episcopal residence is in town. This is only a house which the Bishop occupies temporarily, for the sake of his health. It is a modest house of one story standing very high, with a commanding view of city, harbor, sea, and suburbs. The floors are marble, and the roof is of open rafters, painted blue, and above 20 feet in height; the windows are as large as doors, and the doors as large as gates. The *mayordomo* shows me the parlor, in which are portraits in oil of distinguished scholars and missionaries and martyrs.

On my way back to the city I direct the driver to avoid the disagreeable road by which we came out, and we drive by a cross road, and strike the Paseo de Tacón at its outer end, where is a fountain and statue, and a public garden of the most exquisite flowers, shrubs, and trees; and around them are standing, though it is nearly dark, files of carriages waiting for the promenaders, who are enjoying a walk in the garden. I am able to take the entire drive of the Paseo. It is straight, very wide, with two carriageways and two footways, with rows of trees between, and at three points has a statue and a fountain. One of these statues, if I recollect aright, is of Tacón; one of a Queen of Spain; and one is an allegorical figure. The Paseo is two or three miles in length; reaching from the Campo de Marte, just outside the walls, to the last statue and public garden, on gradually ascending ground, and lined with beautiful villas, and rich gardens full of tropical trees and plants. No city in America has such an avenue as the Paseo de Tacón...

Tomorrow, I am to go, at eight o'clock, either to the church of San Domingo, to hear the military mass, or to the Jesuit church of Belén; for the service of my own church is not publicly celebrated, even at the British consulate, no service but the Roman Catholic being tolerated on the island.

Tonight there is a public *máscara* (mask ball) at the great hall, next door to Le Grand's. My only window is by the side of the numerous windows of the great hall, and all these are wide open; and I should be stifled if I were to close mine. The music is loud and violent, from a very large band, with kettle drums and bass drums and trumpets; and because these do not make noise and uproar enough, leather bands are snapped, at the turns in the tunes. For sleeping, I might as well have been stretched on the bass drum. This tumult of noises, and the heat are wearing and oppressive beyond endurance, as it draws on past midnight, to the small hours; and the servants in the court of the hall seem to be tending at tables of quarrelling men, and to be interminably washing and breaking dishes. After several feverish hours, I light a match and look at my watch. It is nearly five o'clock in the morning. There is an hour to daylight—and will this noise stop before then? The city clocks struck five; the music ceased; and the bells of the convents and monasteries tolled their matins, to call the nuns and monks to their prayers and to the bedsides of the

sick and dying in the hospitals, as the maskers go home from their
revels at this hideous hour of Sunday morning. The servants ceased
their noises, the cocks began to crow and the bells to chime, the
trumpets began to bray, and the cries of the streets broke in before
dawn, and I dropped asleep just as I was thinking sleep past hoping
for; when I am awakened by a knocking at the door, and Antonio
calling, "Usted! Usted! Un caballero quiere ver á Usted!" to find it
half-past nine, the middle of the forenoon, and an ecclesiastic in black
dress and shovel hat, waiting in the passage-way, with a message
from the Bishop.

His Excellency regrets not having seen me the day before, and
invites me to dinner at three o'clock, to meet three or four gentlemen,
an invitation which I accept with pleasure.

I am too late for the mass, or any other religious service, as all
the churches close at ten o'clock. A tepid, soothing bath, at "Los
baños públicos," round the corner, and I spend the morning in my
chamber...

Soon after two o'clock, I take a carriage for the Bishop's. On my
way out I see that the streets are full of Spanish sailors from the
men-of-war, ashore for a holiday, dressed in the style of English
sailors, with wide duck trousers, blue jackets, and straw hats, with
the name of their ship on the front of the hat. All business is going
on as usual, and laborers are at work in the streets and on the houses.

The company consists of the Bishop himself, the Bishop of Puebla
de los Ángeles in Mexico, Father Yuch, the rector of the Jesuit College,
who has a high reputation as a man of intellect, and two young ecclesiastics. Our dinner is well cooked, and in the Spanish style, consisting of fish, vegetables, fruits, and of stewed light dishes, made
up of vegetables, fowls and other meats, a style of cooking well ad-
apted to a climate in which one is very willing to dispense with the
solid, heavy cuts of an English dinner.

The Bishop of Puebla wore the purple, the Bishop of Havana a
black robe with a broad cape, lined with red, and each wore the
Episcopal cross and ring. The others were in simple black cassocks.
The conversation was in French; for, to my surprise, none of the
company could speak English; and being allowed my election between French and Spanish, I chose the former, as the lighter infliction
on my associates.

I am surprised to see what an impression is made on all classes in this country by the pending "Thirty Millions Bill" of Mr. Slidell. It is known to be an Administration measure, and is thought to be the first step in a series which is to end in an attempt to seize the island. Our steamer brought oral intelligence that it had passed the Senate, and it was so announced in the Diario of the day after our arrival, although no newspaper that we brought so stated it. Not only with these clergymen, but with the merchants and others whom I have met since our arrival, foreigners as well as Cubans, this is the absorbing topic. Their future seems to be hanging in doubt, depending on the action of our government, which is thought to have a settled purpose to acquire the island. I suggested that it had not passed the Senate, and would not pass the House; and, at most, was only an authority to the President to make an offer that would certainly be refused. But they looked beyond the form of the act, and regarded it as the first move in a plan, of which, although they could not entirely know the details, they thought they understood the motive.

Joseph J. Dimock

Impressions of Cuba, 1859

Tuesday, February 2, 1859

A pleasant morning but toward noon the weather becomes uncomfortable and blustering. On board steamer, *Empire City*, at twelve o'clock with Cousin Anita. Several friends come down to see us off, but I was in "a state of mind" in consequence of not getting my trunk and carpet bag in which I had laid in a store of conveniences for the voyage such as books, cigars, seidlitz powders etc. The stupid porter at the Metropolitan (though repeatedly directed) took my baggage on board a steamer for Savannah, instead of Havana. All the baggage with me consisted of a bottle of good brandy which Warren Leland placed in my hands on leaving the hotel…

Tuesday, February 8, 1859
Clear and warm, thermometer 78 degrees at noon. Coast of Cuba in sight this afternoon. Cardenas Light and then the *Pan of Matanzas*. All the passengers elated at the prospect of going into Havana tomorrow morning. All up on deck till a late hour. Saw Moro light before turning in.

Friday, February 11
There was a grand serenade at the plaza tonight given to the Captain General by the volunteers of Havana, in honor of his expected departure for the Peninsula. All the *crack* band of the army, the opera troupe etc., joined in vocal and instrumental music. The sight was a brilliant one and we who took ladies with us enjoyed it, for we had the "lindas Americanas." The soldiers' *vivas*, and "long live Isabel and Spain," etc., were coldly received by the masses, and the soldiers *only* cheered while the spectators quietly laughed at the demonstration. It was intended for a great ovation to Concha previous to his departure, but for a political demonstration it was a complete failure. The Captain General was so much cut up by it that he refused to show himself on the balcony to his "ever faithful" subjects as is customary. Concha never goes about the city without his mounted guard of a hundred lancers, and it is evident from the precautions taken by him that he does not consider himself safe without them. The Cubans (*criollos*) say if found alone in the streets he would be assassinated...

Saturday, February 12
The stores here are very small and make but little pretention to style or size. Each store has a name. Not the name of the proprietor for that does not appear, but the store is named according to the fancy of the proprietor without any regard to its adaptation to the business with-in. For instance I have seen "The Angel," "The Flower of Havana," "The Strong Arm," "The Little Rooster," "My Destiny," "The Green Crop," " The First Book of Paris," "The Bomb," "The Bon Ton," "The True Cross," "The Never Die," "The Goats Feet," and many other designations quite as ridiculous...

The quays or wharves of Havana are very superior, beginning at the lower end of the Alameda d'Paula, and all along as far as nearly to the fish market are fine wharves, and mostly covered by a light roof supported by slender columns and built of iron. This is for the protection of merchandise and also of the laborers who are not thereby exposed to the rays of the sun, which are intolerable in the warm season. All vessels lie at the wharf stern to shore and it is a long job to discharge a large cargo by sliding down on planks from the bows to the wharf. All vessels entering must come to anchor in the harbor, which is perfectly safe and commodious, and go through a long series of formalities before they can take their turn for wharfage. The harbor is completely filled with vessels at anchor, and I notice the great proportion of them are American, a great many from "away down East" in Maine. It is estimated that two-thirds of all the shipping entering the port is American. Our trade with the island is immense, and although Cuba is a great market for American goods, yet the difference in favor of Cuba last year was over $5 million.

The enormous tax in the way of duties prevents the importation of many American goods. Our American steamers, with the exception of the *Isabel* running to Charleston, are obliged to anchor at some considerable distance from the city proper, and passengers go to and from the ship in small boats, and in bad weather it is somewhat unpleasant if not a hazardous experiment…

Though the Spanish nation have an open hatred of everything American, yet lately, for some reason, (perhaps the "thirty million" proposition) they seem to treat us with unusual respect. Americans can and do talk here openly of buying Cuba, of annexation and of *manifest destiny* and are only answered by a shrug of incredulous shoulders. Within a few days for the first time in history, our American mail steamers have been saluted by a gun from the flagship of the Spanish Admiral. What this unusual politeness portends I cannot say. A Creole gentleman (Señor E.) tells me they begin to believe in manifest destiny. Certain it is, that the idea of annexation to the States is getting to be very popular here, not only among the Creoles, but among *young* Spaniards who have had an opportunity to become acquainted with American ways and means. Cuba is a garden of the world, and essential to the growth and prosperity of our union and must eventually be with us and of us…

I have spoken heretofore I think of Creoles, a wrong impression exists in the States as to the proper definition of the word "Creole;" many supposing it to imply negro or mixed blood. This is wrong and has been confounded with the Quadroon. By Creole is understood here, all who have been born on the island without regard to sex or color. The white Creoles are denied many privileges allowed to Spanish born, and there seems to be a natural enmity between them. No Creole is allowed to hold any official position either civil or military on the island...

One of the most noted places in Havana is the Cafe Dominica, or coffee house of Señor Dominica. It is a large saloon something in the style of Taylors in Broadway only not as large and clean, for these Spaniards are about the dirtiest people extant. In the centre of a large open courtyard covered by awnings, etc., is a beautiful fountain, with water trickling over the rocks, and the wild aquatic plants of the tropics, trailing from the ledge. Here may be seen at all hours, the Havaneros eating and drinking, for they eat sweetmeats or dulces at any time for they have a terrible sweet tooth, and it is amusing to hear them call for the different American drinks. There are no terms or words in Spanish to express many of them so they call for *brandee punnsch, geen cotell* etc., etc. The favorite beverages of both Spaniards and Creoles seems to be a mixture of eggs and wine, fresh grape juice, *orcharda* (being an emulsion of almonds and sweetened water) *pinales* (a lemonade) and claret in endless profusion. Claret, or a species of it, called *Catalan* wine, is in fact on the table at every meal and drank diluted with water, by old and young of both sexes. It can be bought from 40 to 50 cents a gallon and has an agreeable but pungent flavor, but nearly as strong as brandy when drank clear...

Lottery tickets are offered you everywhere in the hotel, street cafe etc., and everybody buys. The Royal *Lotteria* is provided for by government and it is believed to be managed strictly fair. The highest prize is $100,000 and the lowest a blank. It is drawn on the twentieth of every month and pays a handsome revenue to government.

Friday, February 18
A sugar plantation is called an estate (*Ingenio* — pronounced *yenhanyo*) and the number of boxes of sugar produced is proportionate to the number of hands employed. This estate is a small one comparatively and owns about 100 negroes of all kinds and produces annually some 2,000 boxes of sugar (this includes in the estimate the muscovada sugar and molasses). The cane is ready for cutting about the middle of December, and it is continued until all is cut, generally finishing about the first of May. It is cut just as fast as can be ground and no great amount is left cut and waiting to be ground at any

time. The cane does not require planting except where old and worn lands are broken up to be reworked, and it is not hoed as formerly, but ploughed through with a cultivator. A few days after being cut the new cane commences springing up, so the first cutting this year is the first ready for cutting next season. The cutting of the cane is done by the negroes of both sexes, with a long heavy knife called a *machete*, and the stalks only are put upon the cart to be carried to the mill; the leaves and tops are left upon the field and answer the purpose of manure, except the portion saved for food of the horses and cattle on the place, of which they are very fond, preferring it to corn leaves. Good land lasts for 20 years or more without ploughing, or any artificial manures. The cane is brought to the mill in huge carts, and the grinding is performed by means of a steam engine, which after pressing the juice from the stalk throws off the refuse, which is called *bagasse*, and this after being dried in the sun, constitutes the fuel for fires to boil the juice. The boiler is heated by wood of which there is an abundance on the surrounding hills. The juice is run into huge pans set over a long range or furnace, and then boiled down and passed from one pan to another, till it acquires the proper consistence and is then dipped into tanks to cool. While boiling, the negroes beat it with long wooden paddles, and sing a kind of medley and chant, which is peculiar to the sugarhouse. I could hardly make out the words but it sounded like, "*a — a cha candala e bla — ebla fuerte — echa candala*," etc., etc., which is a cry to the firemen to put on more heat, more fire, etc. This monotonous chant is heard without intermission day and night for the negro cannot work without talking or singing and each new gang take up the same song. After the boiled syrup is partly cooled it is poured into iron cones or tubes to *purge* and packed over with clay to whiten. The molasses is drained through from these tubes and carried off by troughs into a large tank, these to be put into hogsheads. The sugar is carried to the drying house, and when sufficiently cured in the sun, is packed up in boxes and ready for shipping. (These boxes are mostly made in New England and cost here $1 each.) Each box contains from 450 to 500 lbs. and is sold by the box at prices varying with the demand. The average price is about $20 a box. The muscovada or brown sugar is not purged or whitened, and is packed in hogsheads weighing from 1000 to 2000 lbs. each and this sells from $1.00 to $1.50 per *arroba* or 25 cents according to quality. About 300 hogsheads are made here annually, and also about 300 hogsheads of molasses each year, which is taken from the tanks by the distiller at about $12 per hogshead. Some idea may be formed of the quantity of saccharin fluid in the cane, when I say it requires about 500 gallons of cane juice to make one box of sugar, so there are on this place boiled up every year one million gallons of juice.

During the grinding season the negroes are divided into two gangs, in order to work all night, and to avoid the want of fresh hands, changing at midnight. Every 10 days or so the grinding is stopped for two or three days, to give an opportunity to clean the pans, boiler and engine and to give the hands rest. While at work the negroes are continually singing their African melodies and keeping time by beating the boiling sugar of which I believe I have just spoken. They are well treated, and well fed, but as to clothing it is difficult to keep much of anything like clothing on them during the day. They seem contented and if they get enough to eat and occasionally a cigar to smoke they rarely complain. They are constitutionally indolent, and have no more judgment than an animal, consequently there are always some in the hospital. With a good owner (the one here is too indulgent, I think) whipping is rare, but the most common punishment is placing in the stocks for a few hours, or solitary confinement in the calaboose, and fed on bread and water. The negro dreads being alone, and craves companionship, food, etc. When the owner of an estate lives abroad, the whole is under charge of an agent called *administrador*. There are also employed on the estate, an engineer, carpenter, a *mayoral* or overseer, a *majordomo* or clerk and first and second sugar masters. There are also under drovers, etc., and generally negroes, and these are the most tyrannical and cruel of all others. The engineer and carpenter are generally Americans and the others *guajiros* or natives of the island.

Monday, February 21
It is estimated that the number of Spaniards living on the island is from 80,000 to 100,000 souls without including the army and navy. The expense of emigration, the fear of yellow fever, and the uncertainty of getting good situations, keep the yearly emigration down to a small figure, not withstanding the probabilities of making a fortune. They generally come over from Spain, at the insistence of relatives already here, and the general appearance and manners of a

great portion of them, gives a very poor idea of the civilization of the mother country, and even the negroes here seem to look down upon them. The inferiority of the lower classes of Spain, when compared with those of Cuba, is even acknowledged by the Spaniards themselves. They may be seen by the cartload, the same as we see the very poorest class of emigrants coming up from Castle Garden in New York, and their appearance is very similar. They stare about, wondering at everything they see, and are pictures of filth, hunger and nakedness. They are called *sucios blancos* (dirty whites) by the negroes and yet shortly after landing these wretches consider themselves masters of the country, and assume a superiority over the Creoles. They keep steadily in view the prospect of making a fortune, from the highest government official, down to the lowest Catalan fresh from the Penninsula. It is a remarkable fact that those coming to this country throw off their idleness, which is characteristic of their nation, and here become industrious and very economical. Those who are not employed by government (and their name is *legion*), devote themselves to trade, and when as clerks or servants, they have amassed a little capital, they are ready to undertake any kind of trade or speculation from selling rum to negroes, to a dash into the slave trade. They sometimes become *refaccionistas* (or those who sell the crops for the planters and make advances of goods and money) without anything much more than nominal capital, and by charging usurious interest, making false entries, etc., they swell the account so large, that not unfrequently in a few years they find themselves owners of the estates they have been supplying; and then they endeavor to marry some rich lady and finally purchase a title or crop of distinction, for they can be had of all grades and prices, and go back to old Spain a *grandee*...

Saturday, February 26
Up early looking about the Esperanza and after breakfast about ten o'clock, rode into Cardenas with Mr. Fortun... He showed me the better portion of Cardenas and some fine residences in the upper part of the city. Afterward I called at his office and made the acquaintance of several merchants, etc. Met John and Ned toward noon and we lunched etc., together... At three o'clock we take the cars for Recreo, and on the way to the depot we persuade Ned to go up with us and spend the night at Bittun's. On arriving at Recreo we find

Domingo waiting for us with horses. On our way up we had considerable fun with a mettlesome Spaniard who showed more than ordinary national stupidity. I opened a package of New York Sunday weeklies, pictorial papers, etc., which I had taken out from my carpetbag, and found folded in one, a printed slip or handbill of a Broadway merchant, offering Central Park skates at reduced prices, etc. The idea of *such* an advertisement in *this* climate was so ridiculous that I showed it to Ned and we laughed over it, sticking it in my hat band. The Don sitting opposite (apparently an intelligent man too) looked at me very seriously for some time and finally said to Ned, "Advise your friend to take that from his sombrero or he will get into trouble." We all laughed and explained what it meant — an advertisement for *skates* and what skates were used for, etc., but he said he knew all about it and there was no use of our trying to humbug him. He knew skates were used in Holland, but not in the United States, and although he pretended to be able to read English, he said it might *read* skates but it had a double meaning that it *meant* war, and was a proclamation from Buchanan, and if it was not removed from my hat, he would take it off himself. At this Ned bristled up and they had some sharp conversation and ended by Ned taking him roughly by the shoulders and forcing him into his own seat and showing him 10 commandments, doubled up into the shape of a big pair of fists, and told him if he touched my hat he would annihilate him. The brave Spaniard immediately cooled down and apologized, which drew a laugh upon him from several English and American passen-gers, which irritated the Don again, and he said "there were too many Americans here already, and they were coming so fast and wouldn't wait for the 'thirty millions,' etc." He left us at the Pelego station, threatening to complain to the Captain General and also to the Queen if necessary to have all these d—d Americans driven from the island.

Monday, February 28
There is one peculiar custom here not found elsewhere, I think. It is courting at the window. Where the suitor is not admitted to the house on account of not having had an introduction, or where the girl's parents disapprove the acquaintance, she finds means for an interview. Young ladies are not allowed to go out, except in company with a *duenna* and so they have no opportunity of communicating

in public with their lovers, so the admirer posts himself at the window which is nearly on a level with the street, and projecting from the house, and *here* he *makes love* through the bars. If he is likely to be interrupted, she gives him notice and he retires to the next house or the adjoining corner till she gives him the signal to come forward to the window... I have from a seat on the *Alameda d'Paula*, watched some of these outdoor courtships with a good deal of interest, and been much amused by the skill the young lady exhibits to prevent discovery.

Sunday, March 13
The colored population of the island is estimated at about 800,000, in which estimate the free negroes are included, amounting to an insignificant proportion. The free negroes in the town are journeymen laborers; many are artisans, few have shops and fewer still are the proprietors of small houses. It is not uncommon for them to know how to read, and even write; but they generally attain only a very limited knowledge of these important requisites... The slaves in Cuba have certain rights, of which they are deprived in the United States. One of the authorities called the *sindico* sees that these rights are fully enjoyed, and he cannot exact anything from the negroes, though they may possess property. He can compel the owner of the negro to give him permission for three days absence to look for another master without being obliged to assign the cause. If the owner values his negro at too high a price, appraisers are appointed to regulate it. The slave can also at any time give money to his master on account of the price of his freedom and require him to declare what that price is, and it cannot be raised afterwards for any cause. Those who have given $50 or over are called *cortados,* and they are entitled to have certain days to themselves, and are sometimes allowed to work on their own account by paying to the master one *real* daily for each hundred dollars of the price...

Cuba has been called the hot-bed of slavery, and it is in a certain sense true, but I claim as a general thing, the slaves have more privileges than in the States. The slave trade still flourishes (and if reports may be believed it does also in the United States in 1859!) though a much less number are imported than in former years. The effect of this is to raise the price of slaves and procure for them better treatment. An able bodied male slave is now valued at an average of

$1,200 to $1,500, and some good house servants are held at over $2,000. A slave when first landed, is worth if sound from $300 to $500, and as he becomes more acclimated and instructed, for their dull natures require a vast deal of training before they can be brought to any position of usefulness, in doing which the overseers have found kindness to go much farther than harshness. Trifling rewards, for services soon establish a good understanding, and they soon grow very tractable though it is a long time before they understand a word of Spanish. The various African tribes are so strongly marked that there is no difficulty in knowing their nationality. The Congoes and those from the Gold Coast are the most numerous. The former are small, but quick and make good laborers. The Santees, Ashantees, and Carrobalees are larger races, more uneasy and powerful at home, and are more rarely conquered in battle or taken prisoner by the shore tribes in Africa, who sell them to slave factories on the coast. There is a mulatto tribe called Ebroes who make excellent domestic servants. The negroes fresh from Africa called *bozales* are almost pitiful to look up on, and one cannot but feel that however hard their future life may be, it cannot but be an improvement upon their previous life. They are the most filthy, ignorant and degraded of the human species. In fact they are animal in their natures and nothing else, and it seems almost an impossibility that such beings should possess a mind...

Sometimes an epidemic gets among the slaves and sweeps them off by hundreds. There are many reasons for this — their carelessness and imprudence in eating and drinking, their extreme filth, and above all, the fact that medicine sometimes seems to have no visible effect. It takes more than twice as much medicine to affect a negro as it does a white man here, but the reason is a mystery to me. The prevailing sickness among the negroes is diseases of the bowels, and for this reason their food is regularly rationed out to them, but they eat fruit immoderately where it grows in such profusion, and the consequence is, there are always more or less in the hospital.

The slave trade will exist just so long as Spain holds the island, and it is far from suppressed, for only last week Lawton told me of a cargo of over 900 lately landed at St. Juan de los Remedos (near Lavalette's place), and that a cargo is daily expected off his place, which is hardly 50 miles from Cardenas. The government officials and Capitan de Partido are undoubtedly liberally *fee'd* and no difficulty is experienced in landing on the coast. After getting clear of the English and American squadrons on the coast of Africa, it is plain sailing and no obstacles. This too, in the face of the treaty obligations which Spain has with other nations. Our American squadron would do more to suppress the slave trade, and also to protect American interests here, if stationed *around the island of Cuba* and the time will come I imagine when such will be the case.

The importation of Chinese or coolies, is getting to be quite an important item, and there are a great many of them scattered all over the island. Probably from 60 to 75,000 and by some have been estimated as high as 300,000. However, less than 50,000 have been entered at Havana and probably of 75,000 will be a larger estimate. The planter pays the importers about $300, and takes the coolie for *apprenticeship* of eight years, paying him $4 a month (and his board and clothing same as negroes) for his services. At the end of that term the Chinaman goes back to the celestial country at his own expense, or is obliged to hire himself out for another eight years. Consequently they are in reality slaves earning about $50 a year.

Wednesday, March 23
Van Cortland and myself started out at five o'clock this morning on a visit to the Moro, Cabanas, and Punta Forts. We finished the three fortifications by nine o'clock and returned to Madame Almy's in time for breakfast. We took the Punta Fort at *reveille*. It is a small affair directly opposite the Moro on the south side of the entrance of the harbor and mounts I think about 50 guns...

We took a boat from the water gate and worked over to the Moro just as the garrison were being mustered for parade and inspection. By the exercise of a little politeness and *considerable assurance* we obtained permission from the officer in command of the gate to enter and examine the castle. It is a fine looking piece of masonry, built upon solid rock foundation, but I noticed the walls are composed of limestone and rocks of coral formations, being quite soft and friable. Also that a great portion which appear very strong and grand from the harbor, is plaster work mixed with old tiles and whitewashed handsomely, but hardly able to resist the influence of mortars and Dahlgren guns... We were allowed to go up to the telegraph station and from there to the top of the lighthouse which is a fine stone structure inside the walls of the castle and was erected by Captain

General O'Donnell in 1844. The view from the lighthouse is un-surpassed in Cuba. The city harbor of Havana can be seen at a glance, and the white walls of the fortification, around the city, were glisten-ing in the rays of the morning sun, which was just rising as we reached the summit. Looking inland the eye reaches over a vast ex-tent of level country looking green and beautiful with the ever waving palm, standing guard over the surrounding fields. The view toward the sea is grand, and on a clear day the Florida Keys can be distinctly seen with the aid of a glass. We counted about 20 sails coming in, from a Prussian 90 gun frigate down to a little Yankee schooner scudding before the morning breeze. Right from under the walls came fast a trim looking mail steamer with our flag flying and at first we supposed it to be the *Empire City*, due yesterday, but a second glance at her size, engine, etc., convinced me to the contrary and we soon ascertained her to be the steamer *Granada*...

On descending into the fort we were allowed by the officer who admitted us to look at the different kinds of arms used, rifles, etc., and as we took an interest in these matters, we became quite sociable with our kind entertainer, and although we avowed ourselves *Ameri-canos* and *filibusteros*, he refused to believe it, with the characteristic shrug, and offered to show us the dungeons, etc., below, and the subterranean passage to the Cabanas. Want of time obliged us to decline, and he gave us a *recommendado* to the officer commanding the gate of the Cabanas fortress. We made a hasty run thro' the Cabanas, and as the sun was getting warm we took a boat soon for the other side and made for our hotel. The Cabanas is much larger than the Moro, and when fully manned, requires a garrison of 2,000 men. I think it mounts about 300 guns. It is in about the same condi-tion as the Moro and built in a similar style, and protected in the rear by a succession of batteries rising up one above the other, on the hills. But I doubt not a few Yankees, with our Engineer Corps, could capture both these famous forts, in a few days at most...

Have been busy all day having a *last look* at all the lions of Havana, and calling on some few friends I have made here saying "adios," for our steamer will surely be here within a few hours.

Thursday, March 24
The distant view of the *Empire City* just beginning to steam up, reminds me that in a few hours I must bid farewell to these delicious

shores of Cuba, with all their features of enchantment, where all nature is beautiful, and where mere existence is a positive luxury. I might fill pages of statistics showing its wonderful fertility; but words cannot express or give adequate idea of what it is; it must be seen to be appreciated... My short stay here seems like a dream; but it is a dream of too bright things to be forgotten. The groves of oranges and palm, the odor of the thousand sweet flowers, the cool nights and sunny days of the tropics, smiling skies and laughing waters, the volantes, military parades, the Plaza d'Armas, and the music of the splendid band each evening, the *paseo* and the bright eyed señoritas, the gardens and fountains — the beautiful harbor of Havana, guarded by its grim fortresses and batteries, and the country with broad fields of sugarcane and its gardens of coffee and tobacco — the long rides through the savannahs and thick woods loaded with the richest and choicest of flora's offerings — all these and a thousand other pleasant memories come trooping through the mind as my thoughts turn homeward. May I live to see this favored island represented by one of the galaxy of stars which glisten in the blue field of the flag of the free.

John Muir

Havana, 1868

One day in January I climbed to the housetop to get a view of another of the fine sunsets of this land of flowers. The landscape was a strip of clear Gulf water, a strip of sylvan coast, a tranquil company of shell and coral keys, and a gloriously colored sky without a threatening cloud. All the winds were hushed and the calm of the heavens was as profound as that of the palmy islands and their encircling waters. As I gazed from one to another of the palm-crowned keys, enclosed by the sunset-colored dome, my eyes chanced to rest upon the fluttering sails of a Yankee schooner that was threading the tortuous channel in the coral reef leading to the harbor of Cedar Keys. "There," thought I, "perhaps I may sail in that pretty white moth." She proved to be the schooner *Island Belle*.

One day soon after her arrival I went over the key to the harbor, for I was now strong enough to walk. Some of her crew were ashore after water. I waited until their casks were filled, and went with them to the vessel in their boat. Ascertained that she was ready to sail with her cargo of lumber for Cuba. I engaged passage on her for 25 dollars, and asked her sharp-visaged captain when he would sail. "Just as soon," said he, "as we get a north wind. We have had northers enough when we did not want them, and now we have this dying breath from the south."

Hurrying back to the house, I gathered my plants, took leave of my kind friends, and went aboard, and soon, as if to calm the captain's complaints, Boreas came foaming loud and strong. The little craft was quickly trimmed and snugged, her inviting sails spread open, and away she dashed to her ocean home like an exulting war-horse to the battle. Islet after islet speedily grew dim and sank beneath the horizon. Deeper became the blue of the water, and in a few hours all of Florida vanished.

This excursion on the sea, the first one after 20 years in the woods, was of course exceedingly interesting, and I was full of hope, glad to be once more on my journey to the South. Boreas increased in power and the *Island Belle* appeared to glory in her speed and managed her full-spread wings as gracefully as a sea-bird. In less than a day our norther increased in strength to the storm point. Deeper and wider became the valleys, and yet higher the hills of the round plain of water. The flying jib and gaff topsails were lowered and mainsails close-reefed, and our deck was white with broken wave-tops.

"You had better go below," said the captain. "The Gulf Stream, opposed by this wind, is raising a heavy sea and you will be sick. No landsman can stand this long." I replied that I hoped the storm would be as violent as his ship could bear, that I enjoyed the scenery of such a sea so much that it was impossible to be sick, that I had long waited in the woods for just such a storm, and that, now that the precious thing had come, I would remain on deck and enjoy it. "Well," said he, "if you can stand this, you are the first landsman I ever saw that could."

I remained on deck, holding on by a rope to keep from being washed overboard, and watched the behavior of the *Belle* as she dared nobly on; but my attention was mostly directed among the glorious fields of foam-topped waves. The wind had a mysterious voice and carried nothing now of the songs of birds or of the rustling of palms and fragrant vines. Its burden was gathered from a stormy expanse of crested waves and briny tangles. I could see no striving in those magnificent wave-motions, no raging; all the storm was apparently inspired with nature's beauty and harmony. Every wave was obedient and harmonious as the smoothest ripple of a forest lake, and after dark all the water was phosphorescent like silver fire, a glorious sight.

Our luminous storm was all too short for me. Cuba's rock-waves loomed above the white waters early in the morning. The sailors, accustomed to detect the faintest land line, pointed out well-known guiding harbor-marks back of the Morro Castle long before I could see them through the flying spray. We sailed landward for several hours, the misty shore becoming gradually more earthlike. A flock of white-plumaged ships was departing from the Havana harbor, or, like us, seeking to enter it. No sooner had our little schooner flapped her sails in the lee of the Castle than she was boarded by a swarm of daintily dressed officials who were good-naturedly and good-gesturedly making all sorts of inquiries, while our busy captain, paying little attention to them, was giving orders to his crew.

The neck of the harbor is narrow and it is seldom possible to sail in to appointed anchorage without the aid of a steam tug. Our captain wished to save his money, but after much profitless tacking was compelled to take the proffered aid of steam, when we soon reached our quiet mid-harbor quarters and dropped anchor among ships of every size from every sea.

I was still 400 or 500 yards from land and could determine no plant in sight excepting the long arched leaf banners of the banana and the palm, which made a brave show on the Morro Hill. When we were approaching the land, I observed that in some places it was distinctly yellow, and I wondered while we were yet some miles distant whether the color belonged to the ground or to sheets of flowers. From our harbor home I could now see that the color was plant-gold. On one side of the harbor was a city of these yellow plants; on the other, a city of yellow stucco houses, narrowly and confusedly congregated.

"Do you want to go ashore?" said the captain to me. "Yes," I replied, "but I wish to go to the plant side of the harbor." "Oh, well," he said, "come with me now. There are some fine squares and gardens in the city, full of all sorts of trees and flowers. Enjoy these today, and some other day we will all go over the Morro Hill with you and gather shells. All kinds of shells are over there; but these yellow slopes that you see are covered only with weeds."

We jumped into the boat and a couple of sailors pulled us to the thronged, noisy wharf. It was Sunday afternoon, the noisiest day of a Havana week. Cathedral bells and prayers in the forenoon, theaters and bull-fight bells and bellowings in the afternoon! Lowly whispered prayers to the saints and the Virgin, followed by shouts of praise or reproach to bulls and matadors!

I made free with fine oranges and bananas and many other fruits. Pineapple I had never seen before. Wandered about the narrow streets, stunned with the babel of strange sounds and sights; went gazing, also, among the gorgeously flowered garden squares, and then waited among some boxed merchandise until our captain, detained by business, arrived. Was glad to escape to our little schooner *Belle* again, weary and heavy laden with excitement and tempting fruits.

As night came on, a thousand lights starred the great town. I was now in one of my happy dreamlands, the fairest of West India islands. But how, I wondered, shall I be able to escape from this great city confusion? How shall I reach nature in this delectable land? Consulting my map, I longed to climb the central mountain range of the island and trace it through all its forests and valleys and over its summit peaks, a distance of 700 or 800 miles. But alas! though out of Florida swamps, fever was yet weighing me down, and a mile of city walking was quite exhausting. The weather too was oppressively warm and sultry.

January 16
During the few days since our arrival the sun usually has risen unclouded, pouring down pure gold, rich and dense, for one or two hours. Then island-like masses of white-edged cumuli suddenly appeared, grew to storm size, and in a few minutes dis-charged rain in tepid splashing bucketfuls, accompanied with high wind. This was followed by a short space of calm, half-cloudy sky, delightfully fragrant with flowers, and again the air would become hot, thick, and sultry.

This weather, as may readily be perceived, was severe to one so weak and feverish, and after a dozen trials of strength over the Morro Hill and along the coast northward for shells and flowers, I was sadly compelled to see that no enthusiasm could enable me to walk to the interior. So I was obliged to limit my researches to within 10 or 12 miles of Havana. Captain Parsons offered his ship as my head-quarters, and my weakness prevented me from spending a single night ashore.

The daily programme for nearly all the month that I spent here was about as follows: After breakfast a sailor rowed me ashore on the north side of the harbor. A few minutes' walk took me past the Morro Castle and out of sight of the town on a broad cactus common, about as solitary and untrodden as the tangles of Florida. Here I zigzagged and gathered prizes among unnumbered plants and shells along the shore, stopping to press the plant specimens and to rest in the shade of vine-heaps and bushes until sundown. The happy hours stole away until I had to return to the schooner. Either I was seen by the sailors who usually came for me, or I hired a boat to take me back. Arrived, I reached up my press and a big handful of flowers, and with a little help climbed up the side of my floating home.

Refreshed with supper and rest, I recounted my adventures in the vine tangles, cactus thickets, sunflower swamps, and along the shore among the breakers. My flower specimens, also, and pocketfuls of shells and corals had to be reviewed. Next followed a cool, dreamy hour on deck amid the lights of the town and the various vessels coming and departing.

Many strange sounds were heard: the vociferous, unsmotherable bells, the heavy thundering of cannon from the Castle, and the shouts of the sentinels in measured time. Combined they made the most incessant sharp-angled mass of noise that I ever was doomed to hear. Nine or ten o'clock found me in a small bunk with the harbor wave-lets tinkling outside close to my ear. The hours of sleep were filled with dreams of heavy heat, of fruitless efforts for the disentanglement of vines, or of running from curling breakers back to the Morro, etc. Thus my days and nights went on…

Havana abounds in public squares, which in all my random strolls throughout the big town I found to be well watered, well cared for, well planted, and full of exceedingly showy and interesting plants, rare even amid the exhaustless luxuriance of Cuba. These squares also contained fine marble statuary and were furnished with seats in the shadiest places. Many of the walks were paved instead of graveled.

The streets of Havana are crooked, labyrinthic, and exceedingly narrow. The sidewalks are only about a foot wide. A traveler experiences delightful relief when, heated and wearied by raids through the breadth of the dingy yellow town, dodging a way through crowds of men and mules and lumbering carts and carriages, he at length finds shelter in the spacious, dustless, cool, flowery squares; still more when, emerging from all the din and darkness of these lanelike streets, he suddenly finds himself out in the middle of the harbor, inhaling full-drawn breaths of the sea breezes.

The interior of the better houses which came under my observation struck me with the profusion of dumpy, ill-proportioned pillars at the entrances and in the halls, and with the spacious open-fielded appearance of their enclosed square house-gardens or courts. Cubans in general appear to me superfinely polished, polite, and agreeable in society, but in their treatment of animals they are cruel. I saw more downright brutal cruelty to mules and horses during the few weeks I stayed there than in my whole life elsewhere. Live chickens and hogs are tied in bunches by the legs and carried to market thus, slung on a mule. In their general treatment of all sorts of animals they seem to have no thought for them beyond cold-blooded, selfish interest.

In tropical regions it is easy to build towns, but it is difficult to subdue their armed and united plant inhabitants, and to clear fields and make them blossom with breadstuff. The plant people of temperate regions, feeble, unarmed, unallied, disappear under the trampling feet of flocks, herds, and man, leaving their homes to enslavable plants which follow the will of man and furnish him with food. But the armed and united plants of the tropics hold their rightful kingdom plantfully, nor, since the first appearance of Lord Man, have they ever suffered defeat.

A large number of Cuba's wild plants circle closely about Havana. In five minutes' walk from the wharf I could reach the undisturbed settlements of Nature. The field of the greater portion of my rambling researches was a strip of rocky common, silent and unfrequented by anybody save an occasional beggar at Nature's door asking a few roots and seeds. This natural strip extended 10 miles along the coast northward, with but few large-sized trees and bushes, but rich in magnificent vines, cacti-composites, leguminous plants, grasses, etc. The wild flowers of this seaside field are a happy band, closely joined in splendid array. The trees shine with blossoms and with light reflected from the leaves. The individuality of the vines is lost in trackless, interlacing, twisting, overheaping union.

Our American "South" is rich in flowery vines. In some districts almost every tree is crowned with them, aiding each other in grace and beauty. Indiana, Kentucky, and Tennessee have the grapevine in predominant numbers and development. Farther south dwell the greenbriers and countless leguminous vines. A vine common among the Florida islets, perhaps belonging to the dogbane family, overruns live-oaks and palmettos, with frequently more than a hundred stems twisted into one cable. Yet in no section of the South are there such complicated and such gorgeously flowered vine-tangles as flourish in armed safety in the hot and humid wild gardens of Cuba.

The longest and the shortest vine that I found in Cuba were both leguminous. I have said that the harbor side of the Morro Hill is clothed with tall yellow-flowered composites through which it is difficult to pass. But there are smooth, velvety lawnlike patches in these *Compositae* forests. Coming suddenly upon one of these open places, I stopped to admire its greenness and smoothness, when I observed a sprinkling of large papilionaceous blossoms among the short green grass. The long composites that bordered this little lawn were entwined and almost smothered with vines which bore similar corollas in tropic abundance.

I at once decided that these sprinkled flowers had been blown off the encompassing tangles and had been kept fresh by dew and by spray from the sea. But, on stooping to pick one of them up, I was surprised to find that it was attached to Mother Earth by a short, prostrate, slender hair of a vine stem, bearing, besides the one large blossom, a pair or two of linear leaves. The flower weighed more than stem, root, and leaves combined. Thus, in a land of creeping and twining giants, we find also this charming, diminutive simplicity — the vine reduced to its lowest terms.

The longest vine, prostrate and untwined like its little neighbor, covers patches of several hundred square yards with its countless branches and close growth of upright, trifoliate, smooth green leaves. The flowers are as plain and unshowy in size and color as those of the sweet peas of gardens. The seeds are large and satiny. The whole plant is noble in its motions and features, covering the ground with a depth of unconfused leafage which I have never seen equaled by any other plant. The extent of leaf-surface is greater, I think, than that of a large Kentucky oak. It grows, as far as my observation has reached, only upon shores, in a soil composed of broken shells and corals, and extends exactly to the water-line of the highest-reaching waves. The same plant is abundant in Florida.

The cacti form an important part of the plant population of my ramble ground. They are various as the vines, consisting now of a diminutive joint or two hid in the weeds, now rising into bushy trees, wide-topped, with trunks a foot in diameter, and with glossy, dark-green joints that reflect light like the silex-varnished palms. They are planted for fences, together with the Spanish bayonet and agave.

In one of my first walks I was laboriously scrambling among some low rocks gathering ferns and vines, when I was startled by finding my face close to a great snake, whose body was disposed carelessly like a castaway rope among the weeds and stones. After escaping and coming to my senses, I discovered that the snake was a member of the vegetable kingdom, capable of no dangerous amount of locomotion, but possessed of many a fang, and prostrate as though under the curse of Eden, "Upon thy belly shalt thou go and dust shalt thou eat."

One day, after luxuriating in the riches of my Morro pasture, and pressing many new specimens, I went down to the bank of brilliant wave-washed shells to rest awhile in their beauty, and to watch the breakers that a powerful norther was heaving in splendid rank along the coral boundary. I gathered pocketfuls of shells, mostly small but fine in color and form, and bits of rosy coral. Then I amused myself by noting the varying colors of the waves and the different forms of their curved and blossoming crests. While thus alone and free it was interesting to learn the richly varied songs, or what we mortals call the roar, of expiring breakers. I compared their variation with the different distances to which the broken wave-water reached landward in its farthest-flung foam-wreaths, and endeavored to form some idea of the one great song sounding forever all around the white-blooming shores of the world.

Rising from my shell seat, I watched a wave leaping from the deep and coming far up the beveled strand to bloom and die in a mass of white. Then I followed the spent waters in their return to the blue deep, wading in their spangled, decaying fragments until chased back up the bank by the coming of another wave. While thus playing half studiously, I discovered in the rough, beaten deathbed of the wave a little plant with closed flowers. It was crouching in a hollow of the brown wave-washed rock, and one by one the chanting, dying waves rolled over it. The tips of its delicate pink petals peered above the clasping green calyx. "Surely," said I, as I stooped over it for a moment, before the oncoming of another wave, "surely you cannot be living here! You must have been blown from some warm bank, and rolled into this little hollow crack like a dead shell." But, running back after every retiring wave, I found that its roots were wedged into a shallow wrinkle of the coral rock, and that this wave-beaten chink was indeed its dwelling-place.

I had oftentimes admired the adaptation displayed in the structure of the stately dulse and other seaweeds, but never thought to find a highbred flowering plant dwelling amid waves in the stormy, roaring domain of the sea. This little plant has smooth globular leaves, fleshy and translucent like beads, but green like those of other land plants. The flower is about five eighths of an inch in diameter, rose-purple, opening in calm weather, when deserted by the waves. In general appearance it is like a small portulaca. The strand, as far as I walked it, was luxuriantly fringed with woody *Compositae,* two or three feet in height, their tops purple and golden with a profusion of flowers. Among these I discovered a small bush whose yellow flowers were ideal; all the parts were present regularly alternate and in fives, and all separate, a plain harmony.

When a page is written over but once it may be easily read; but if it be written over and over with characters of every size and style, it soon becomes unreadable, although not a single confused meaningless mark or thought may occur among all the written characters to mar its perfection. Our limited powers are similarly perplexed and overtaxed in reading the inexhaustible pages of nature, for they are written over and over uncountable times, written in characters of every size and color, sentences composed of sentences, every part of a character a sentence. There is not a fragment in all nature, for every relative fragment of one thing is a full harmonious unit in itself. All together form the one grand palimpsest of the world.

One of the most common plants of my pasture was the agave. It is sometimes used for fencing. One day, in looking back from the top of the Morro Hill, as I was returning to the *Island Belle*, I chanced to observe two poplarlike trees about 25 feet in height. They were growing in a dense patch of cactus and vine-knotted sunflowers. I was anxious to see any-thing so homelike as a poplar, and so made haste towards the two strange trees, making a way through the cactus and sunflower jungle that protected them. I was surprised to find that what I took to be poplars were agaves in flower, the first I had seen. They were almost out of flower, and fast becoming wilted at the approach of death. Bulbs were scattered about, and a good many still remained on the branches, which gave it a fruited appearance.

The stem of the agave seems enormous in size when one considers that it is the growth of a few weeks. This plant is said to make a mighty effort to flower and mature its seeds and then to die of exhaustion. Now there is not, so far as I have seen, a mighty effort or the need of one, in wild Nature. She accomplishes her ends without unquiet effort, and perhaps there is nothing more mighty in the development of the flower-stem of the agave than in the development of a grass panicle.

Havana has a fine botanical garden. I spent pleasant hours in its magnificent flowery arbors and around its shady fountains. There is a palm avenue which is considered wonderfully stately and beautiful, 50 palms in two straight lines, each rigidly perpendicular. The smooth round shafts, slightly thicker in the middle, appear to be productions of the lathe, rather than vegetable stems. The 50 arched crowns, inimitably balanced, blaze in the sunshine like heaps of stars that have fallen from the skies. The stems were about 60 or 70 feet in height, the crowns about 15 feet in diameter.

Along a stream-bank were tall, waving bamboos, leafy as willows, and infinitely graceful in wind gestures. There was one species of palm, with immense bipinnate leaves and leaflets fringed, jagged, and one-sided, like those of *Adiantum*. Hundreds of the most gorgeous-flowered plants, some of them large trees, belonging to the *Leguminosae*. Compared with what I have before seen in artificial flower-gardens, this is past comparison the grandest. It is a perfect metropolis of the brightest and most exuberant of garden plants, watered by handsome fountains, while graveled and finely bordered walks slant and curve in all directions, and in all kinds of fanciful playground styles, more like the fairy gardens of the Arabian Nights than any ordinary man-made pleasure-ground.

In Havana I saw the strongest and the ugliest negroes that I have met in my whole walk. The stevedores of the Havana wharf are muscled in true giant style, enabling them to tumble and toss ponderous casks and boxes of sugar weighing hundreds of pounds as if they were empty. I heard our own brawny sailors, after watching them at work a few minutes, express unbounded admiration of their strength, and wish that their hard outbulging muscles were for sale. The countenances of some of the negro orange-selling dames express a devout good-natured ugliness that I never could have conceived any arrangement of flesh and blood to be capable of. Besides oranges they sold pineapples, bananas, and lottery tickets.

★

After passing a month on this magnificent island, and finding that my health was not improving, I made up my mind to push on...

When I was resting in one of the Havana gardens, I noticed in a New York paper an advertisement of cheap fares to California. I consulted Captain Parsons concerning a passage to New York, where I could find a ship for California. At this time none of the California ships touched at Cuba.

"Well," said he, pointing toward the middle of the harbor, "there is a trim little schooner loaded with oranges for New York, and these little fruiters are fast sailers. You had better see her captain about a passage, for she must be about ready to sail." So I jumped into the dinghy and a sailor rowed me over to the fruiter. Going aboard, I inquired for the captain, who appeared on deck and readily agreed to carry me to New York for 25 dollars. Inquiring when he would sail, "Tomorrow morning at daylight," he replied, "if this norther slacks a little; but my papers are made out, and you will have to see the American consul to get permission to leave on my ship."

I immediately went to the city, but was unable to find the consul, whereupon I determined to sail for New York without any formal leave. Early next morning, after leaving the *Island Belle* and bidding Captain Parsons good-bye, I was rowed to the fruiter and got aboard. Notwithstanding the north wind was still as boisterous as ever, our Dutch captain was resolved to face it, confident in the strength of his all-oak little schooner.

Vessels leaving the harbor are stopped at the Morro Castle to have their clearance papers examined; in particular, to see that no runaway slaves were being carried away. The officials came alongside our little ship, but did not come aboard. They were satisfied by a glance at the consul's clearance paper, and with the declaration of the captain, when asked whether he had any negroes, that he had "not a d—d one." "All right, then," shouted the officials, "farewell! A pleasant voyage to you!" As my name was not on the ship's papers, I stayed below, out of sight, until I felt the heaving of the waves and knew that we were fairly out on the open sea. The Castle towers, the hills, the palms, and the wave-white strand, all faded in the distance, and our mimic sea-bird was at home in the open stormy gulf, curtsying to every wave and facing bravely to the wind.

Walter Goodman

An Enchanted Painter;
A Taste of Cuban Prison Life, 1873

An Enchanted Painter

It is not always easy to secure the services of a better class of model than our peripatetic of the pavement. Before we can induce such a person to walk into our studio, many arts, unconnected with our calling, must be employed, especially if the object of our solicitation happen to be young and fair. Having directed our professional gaze upon such a Señorita, it behoves us first to visit her family, and make friends with her parents, brothers or sisters, in order that their consent may be easily and naturally obtained. Thus, when I cast my artistic eye upon the pretty Perpetua, I have to proceed with extreme caution, lest her parents should misinterpret the nature of my demand. For Perpetua belongs to the octoroon "species" of mulatto. Her father is a white man, and her mother is a free-born quadroon-woman, and they reside with their daughter in an humble dwelling near our studio. Don Ramon being a small tobacconist, and his wife, Doña Choncha, a laundress, we have sometimes patronised the little family, and in this manner I make the acquaintance of my future model. It is, however, far from easy to persuade the old lady that my admiration for her daughter is wholly confined to the pictur-esque; for when I broach the model-subject, Doña Choncha smiles incredulously, and says she will consult her friends. While she is doing so, an extraordinary revelation respecting the brown old dame is made to me by Mateo, the *sereno* or watchman of our district.

Armed with a pike, lantern, revolver, and coil of rope for pinion-ing purposes, the watchman wanders about our neighbourhood, halting every quarter of an hour to blow a shrill whistle to inform the inhabitants of the time of night, and whether it is *sereno* (fine) or *nublado* (cloudy).

One dark night the *sereno* pauses before our balcony, and after assuring the somnolent, in recitative, that it is "three-quarters past eleven and *nu-bla-do!*" approaches me, and in a mysterious whisper enquires whether I carry *contradaños*, or charms against evil, about my person. Finding that I do not possess such articles, the watchman recommends me to apply without delay for a talisman or two. Raw mustard, powdered glass, and sulphur, he says, are highly effectual as charms. At that very moment Mateo's pockets are full of these safeguards, and when threatened with any danger, he has only to sprinkle around him some of the antidote against evil.

The watchman then tells me that Doña Choncha is in league with *brujas* (witches), and that if I continue to visit at her house I shall do well to take the precautions he has suggested.

Mateo is himself a firm believer in the Black Art, and gives me some interesting particulars respecting a secret society of sorcerers, who hold certain midnight revels in an empty saloon of a house somewhere in the town. There is a kind of freemason mystery attach-ed to their proceedings, and none but members are in the secret. It appears, however, that their dark deeds consist chiefly in a dead-of-night dance around a defunct *majá*, or enchanted snake, by a num-ber of people, most of whom are attired in nature's vestments.

The watchman likewise tells me that the practice of witchcraft in Cuba is sometimes attended with serious and fatal consequences, and that crimes of the worst description are frequently the result of it. An individual unwittingly takes his neighbour's life in obedience to commands from a sanguinary sorcerer, who requires a certain weight of human blood to complete the ingredients of an enchanted preparation. "Bring me a couple of handfuls of hair, and four ounces of blood from Fulano," says the weird, who has been applied to for spiritual absolution, "and I will prepare you a *contradaño* — a charm — that shall rid you of your evil genius, and help you out of your present difficulty." Fulano objects to part with his "personal" property, when the request is made to him in a friendly way; so he gets a hard knock on the head one day, when he least expects it, and if he escapes with his life he is lucky.

Such instances of witchcraft as these, the *sereno* says, are found only among the coloured population of Cuba, and when discovered the perpetrators of the nefarious acts are brought to justice and severely punished; but belief in necromancy exists even among the more enlightened inhabitants of Cuba, and it is far from uncommon to hear of highly respectable whites taking part in the practice of it.

Mateo then gives me his own personal experiences of the Black Art as a warning against the danger which, he says, will surely threaten me if I continue to visit the tobacconist family.

The watchman assures me that for many long weeks he had laboured under the depressing influence of a spell. The unfortunate occurrence began with an anonymous letter conveying the unwelcome information that a certain enemy of Mateo's was engaged in brewing some dreadful mischief for his especial benefit. In his professional capacity, the watchman has more than one foe in the town, and it is therefore difficult to "spot," and afterwards capture, the actual offender. The warning letter, however, admonishes him that so long as he does not walk in a certain locality, no harm to him can possibly accrue. It is not easy for Mateo to avoid the indicated thoroughfare, as it happens to come exactly within our watchman's beat at night; but he surmounts the obstacle at the risk of incurring his employers' displeasure, by exchanging beats with a brother watchman. The irregular act is, however, made known to the authorities, and Mateo is threatened with instant dismissal if he persists in avoiding the street in question. Fortunately, the *sereno* receives a second missive from the anonymous correspondent, containing the assurance that there is still hope for immediate and radical disenchantment if Mateo will only follow the writer's advice. This consists, first of all, in depositing a piece of coin under the door of his correspondent's habitation. At an early hour, the money will disappear through some unseen agency, and will afterwards be consigned to a disenchanting locality in the Cuban bay. The *sereno* is next enjoined to examine the lining of his brand new panama, which he has lately purchased to wear only on festive occasions. If all goes well, he will assuredly discover certain black pins and human hairs crossed, entwined and affixed in a peculiar fashion to the crown of his hat. The same evil omens will likewise appear at the ferule end of his gold-knobbed walking-stick. Satisfied that there is "no deception," the proprietor of the enchanted hat and cane wraps up those articles carefully in several folds of paper, according to instructions, and early one Sunday morning deposits the parcel in a certain hole in an undesirable field on the confines of the town.

"When I had done so," concludes the watchman, pausing to inform the inhabitants that it is three-quarters past midnight and *nubla-do!* — "when I had done so, I walked without fear along the forbidden street, and I have walked there in safety ever since!"

The watchman enjoins me to be warned by his story, and once more advises me to provide myself with a few *contradaños*.

"Had I taken the same precautions," observes Mateo, "I should have escaped all my troubles."

"And preserved your panama and gold-headed cane!" I add.

"Past one o'clock and *seren-o!*" sings the watchman as he takes his leave of me.

My interest in the tobacconist's family is considerably increased by what I have heard, and my visits are nonetheless frequent because of the friendly admonitions which I have received. I do not provide myself with the talismans which the *sereno* has recommended; but I watch the old lady's ways more narrowly than I have before done, till I begin at last to detect something like a malignant expression in her shrunken, yellow-brown countenance.

I observe no change in her pretty daughter, though I must confess that in one way, at least, La Perpetua is more "charming" than ever. The young girl is full of her approaching "fiesta," or saint's day, which annual event is to be celebrated by an afternoon ball and early supper at her humble home. The presents she expects to receive in the shape of trays of *dulces* and confectionary will, she assures me, exceed those of the past fiesta. Perpetua is the acknowledged belle of the *barrio,* or district, where she resides, and she has many admirers. But unfortunately the young creole is not so white as her fair complexion would lead one to suppose. Don Ramon is undoubtedly a white man, but his wife belongs to the mulatto tribe, and Perpetua's origin is unquestionably obscure. Still Doña Choncha has great hopes that her pretty daughter will command a white alliance among her husband's friends in spite of this drawback, and it is whispered that the ambitious old dame has her eye upon more than one eligible suitor for her child's whitey-brown hand. Mateo, the watchman — ever hard on Doña Choncha — declares that it is her "evil eye" that is being exercised in Perpetua's behalf; but I heed him not, though I am now more than ever cautious in my behaviour at the tobacconist's.

Whatever truth there may be in the watchman's assertion that I am the object of enchantment, at present I have received no practical evidence of it. When I probe Perpetua privately on the subject, I find that she has little to tell, except that her mother is in the habit of visiting a locality in the town unknown to Perpetua and Don Ramon, and that, upon one occasion, she administered a harmless drug to her daughter, assuring her that it was a protection against cholera.

As for Don Ramon — that good-natured gentleman is altogether a disbeliever in witchcraft, and though he admits that the art is popular among a certain class in Cuba, he is of opinion that the Cuban *bruja,* or witch, is simply a high order of gipsy, whose chief object is pecuniary gain. The government of the country, with its accustomed inertness, has not yet established a law for the suppression of this evil; "and so," says the tobacconist, "sorcery flourishes, and the *brujas* prosper."

I am beginning to abandon all hope of obtaining La Perpetua for a model, when one day I receive an anonymous letter, the handwriting and diction of which seem to be the production of an uninstructed Ethiop. The writer assures me that somebody or other is at present engaged in the useful occupation of working for my complete overthrow and subjugation, and that if I require further particulars on the subject I may easily obtain them for the small consideration of a "punctured peseta" (a coin with a "lucky" hole in it).

When I exhibit the mysterious document to the watchman, that individual is of course highly pleased to find that I have, at last, received some evidence of the existence of such mighty people as *brujas,* and his advice resolves itself, as usual, into sulphur and powdered mustard. He has now not the least doubt that Doña Choncha has made application to the *brujas* for a spell, and he recommends me to pay the peseta asked of me by my anonymous correspondent.

A communication from a live witch is worth all the money demanded for it, and I accordingly place the coin, as directed, in a crevice under my door. Sure enough, it disappears before daylight, and in return I obtain a second sheet of magic manuscript, which, like its predecessor, is unpleasantly greasy to the touch and offensive to the nose; but it is full of information, and concludes with an offer to effect my permanent disenchantment if I will but follow the writer's instructions. If I am disposed to do so, I must first meet the writer, or his deputy, alone in a certain unfrequented locality of the town at a late hour; arming myself with a *contradaño* in the shape of a *media onza*. Thirty-four shillings may appear a high rate for disenchantment, but the watchman assures me that the operation often costs four times that amount, and that if the unknown *bruja* fulfils his promise I shall have made a great bargain. As I do not value my malignant spirit at any price, I decline for the present to avail myself of this opportunity to be relieved of it.

My occupations prevent me from paying my accustomed visits at the tobacconists for some days, but one sunny morning I venture to look in at the little establishment.

Don Ramon, I am told, is passing some weeks at his *vega*, or tobacco farm; but his black assistants are at their wooden benches as usual, rolling tobacco leaves into cigars. I pass through the section of a shop (which has neither wall nor window in front of it) into the inner apartment, usually occupied by Doña Choncha and her daughter, and find the former engaged in sorting tobacco leaves on the brick-floor, and the latter in swaying and fanning herself in a cane rocking-chair. Both ladies salute me respectfully, and make kind enquiries after my health. These formalities over, Doña Choncha collects together her tobacco leaves, and, without a word of explanation, adjourns to the *patio*. For the first time, since my acquaintance with the tobacconist's family, I am left alone with the pretty Perpetua!

All is not well with her weird-looking mother, as I very shortly have reason to find. I have been scarcely 10 minutes in Perpetua's agreeable society, when she is summoned by her mother to the courtyard. Upon her return I am offered some *refresco*, made from the juicy fruit of the *guanabana*.

"Who mixed this drink?" I enquire, after taking a sip of it.

"La máma mixed it," replies Perpetua.

Has the old hag added some infernal drug to the refreshment? I wonder; for there is something besides *guanabana* in the libation!

While I am speculating about this, lo! a strange odour is wafted into the little chamber, and presently some smoke is seen to issue from an aperture in the door.

Is the house on fire? Perpetua is again summoned by Doña Choncha; but before leaving the apartment she begs me not to be alarmed, as it is only her mother at her duties. I would willingly believe what she says, but being sufficiently familiar with the process of drying tobacco leaves, I am convinced that sulphur, hair, mustard, and heaven knows what besides, are not employed in it. The fumes of these burning substances are, however, entering the apartment, and the atmosphere is most oppressive — so much so, that my pulse beats high, and my head begins to swim.

Without waiting another moment, I seize my walking-stick and panama hat, and escape from the enchanted chamber into the street. The hot air does not dispel the giddy feeling which had come over me, and not until I have reached my well-ventilated abode, changed my damp linen, and sponged my fevered body with *aguardiente* and water, do I feel myself again. I am better still after having taken a refreshing siesta in my swinging hammock, in which condition I dream of black pins, burnt hair, raw mustard, and sulphur. When I awake, I examine carefully the lining of my panama, and the ferule end of my walking-stick, to satisfy myself that no burglarious *bruja* has taken advantage of my repose to tamper with my property. But whether it is that my stick and hat are of no great value, or that the defences of our studio are impregnable, no *bruja* has offered to take "charge" of these things by labelling them with their infernal tickets.

My partner, to whom I record the events of the day, is of opinion that if all models are as difficult to secure as La Perpetua, we had better abandon our researches in this direction, and abide by our street criers and mendicants. He also suggests a little landscape-painting by way of variety, and, with this object in view, we plan certain walking expeditions into the surrounding country.

A taste of Cuban Prison Life

I dream that I am Silvio Pellico, that the prisoner of St. Helena is my fellow-captive, and that an apartment belonging to the Spanish Inquisition is our dormitory. Clasps of iron eat their way into our ankles and wrists; gigantic rats share our food; our favourite exercise is swinging head downwards in the air, and our chief recreation is to watch the proceedings of tame spiders.

I awake and find my bed unusually hard. My bed-clothes have vanished, and in their stead are a couple of hard benches, with my wearing apparel rolled up for a pillow. By a dim light I observe that my apartment is remarkably small, bare, damp, and dome-shaped. The window is a barred aperture in the door; is only a foot square, and looks on to the *patio*, or narrow passage, where unlimited wall stares me in the face. Do I still dream, or is this actually one of "le mie prigioni"? I rub my eyes for a third time, and look about the semi-darkened vault. Somebody is snoring. I gaze in the direction whence the sound proceeds, and observe indistinctly an object huddled together in a corner. So, this is no dream, after all; and that heap of sleeping humanity is not Napoleon, but my companion, Nicasio Rodriguez y Boldu.

We are both shut up in one of the subterranean dungeons of the Morro Castle; not the Havana Morro, but the fortress at Santiago de Cuba...

Why are we here?

What were we doing yesterday afternoon?

Well; we were taking a seven miles walk to the Morro Castle, the picturesque neighbourhood of which we had not yet visited, and as the grounds attached to the fortress are always open to the public, we proposed a quiet evening saunter over them.

We had a negro with us, an old and faithful vassal, who at the present moment is enjoying solitary confinement in another part of the fortress. We reached the castle grounds, where a group of Spanish *militares* were seated. We gave them the "Buenas tardes;" they returned our salute, and their chief, who was no less a personage than the commandant of the Morro, offered us refreshment, and permitted us to wander about the grounds. In our ramble we paused here and there to admire the picturesque "bits" of scenery which, at every turn of a winding road, broke upon our view. By a narrow path cut in the grey rock we descended to the sea-shore, and stood before the entrance of the Cuban harbour. We watched the French packet as she steamed into port on her way to the town, and saw the gun fired which announced her arrival. The steamer was so near, that we could scan the faces of everybody on board, and hear enthusiastic congratulations on their safe arrival after their tedious voyage. The skipper conferred with the Morro guard. What was the ship's name? Where did she hail from? Who was her captain? Where was she bound for? A needless demand, I thought, seeing that there is no water navigable beyond the town; but it was in strict conformity with Spanish regulations.

As evening advanced, we prepared to return to our temporary home, where a good dinner doubtless awaited us, with a cup of café noir to follow, and correspondence — ah! my friends never missed a mail — to open and to devour.

"Alto allá!" The ominous command to halt where we stood, still rings in my ear. A party of soldiers, with pointed muskets and fixed bayonets, ran with all speed in our direction.

"Car-amba!" Were we the object of their precipitation? We were! They conducted us to an eminence, where stood a podgy, high-shouldered, short-necked man with a squeaky interrogative voice and gold spectacles. This was the commandant. Without explanation, that officer, in brief words, ordered us to be arrested.

The soldiers obeyed. They bandaged our eyes with handkerchiefs. They led us along hollow-sounding alleys; beneath echoing archways; down scores of stone steps; through mouldy passages. Lower yet, where a strong flavour of cooking assailed our sense of smell. A couple more downward flights, and then we paused — heard a jingling of big keys, an opening of ponderous doors — and here we were.

Here, in a subterranean vault, I know not how many feet below sunlight. The air is close and vaporous; the domed chamber is damp and musty. They have divested us of all our portable property save a few cigarettes which we have secreted in a dark corner, and there is nothing to be had in the way of refreshment for love or money.

Yes, for money. I have bribed the sentinel, who occasionally eclipses our square of window, with all my ready cash, and he has brought us contraband cups of weak coffee. Will he treat our dark domestic as well? We try him, and find that he won't.

What's o'clock? We have no means of ascertaining this, as Phoebus, who might have suggested the time of day, is a long way out of sight. Our sentinel says it is early morning.

Hark! A sound of many footsteps; a rattling of arms and keys. Enter our military jailer with a dozen soldiers to release us from our present quarters. Our eyes are bandaged as before, and after passing up several flights of steps in another direction, our sight is restored: the scene changes, and we are discovered, like the Prince of Denmark, upon another part of the platform. Our faithful vassal is with us, looking as much like a ghost as it is possible for a negro to appear. They have tied his arms behind him with cords, and serve us in the same manner; while eight soldiers encircle us at respectful distances, and deliberately proceed to load their weapons. The negro trembles with affright, and falls on his knees. Misericordia! they are going to shoot us, he thinks; for he is ignorant of the Spanish custom of loading in the presence of the prisoner before escorting him from one jail to another.

To another? Santo Dios! Then we are prisoners still?

I think of the victim of Santa Margherita and his many prisons, and begin to wonder how many years of incarceration we shall experience.

"En marcha!" Eight *militares* and a sergeant place us in their midst, and in this way we march to town, a distance of seven miles. Our sergeant proves to be more humane than his superior, and on the uneven road pauses to screw up cigarettes for us, and, in consideration of our helpless condition, even places them in our mouths.

It is Sunday morning, and when we reach the town all good Catholics have been to high mass, and are parading the narrow thoroughfare dressed in fashionable attire. Crowds gather around us and speculate as to the particular crime we are guilty of; and, to tell the truth, our appearance is by no means respectable. Have we shot the commandant? Undermined the Morro? Poisoned the garrison? Have we headed a negro conspiracy, or joined a gang of pirates? Friends whom we recognise on our way endeavour to interrogate us, but are interrupted by the sergeant. We halt before the governor's house; but his excellency is not yet out of bed, and may not be disturbed. So we proceed to the town jail, where everybody is stirring and where they are happy to see us, and receive us with open doors. A dozen policemen, dressed in brown-holland coats, trimmed with yellow braid and silver buttons, with panama hats, revolvers, and short Roman swords, are seated on benches at the prison entrance. Passing them, we are hurried into a whitewashed chamber, where a frowning functionary, in brown-holland and silver lace, with a panama on his head, and a long cigar in his mouth, sits at a desk scribbling something on stamped paper. He pauses to examine and peruse a large letter which our sergeant hands him, and which contains a statement of our arrest, with full particulars of our misdeeds. The document is folded in official fashion, is written, regardless of economy, with any quantity of margin, and is terminated by a tremendous signature, accompanied by an elaborate flourish, which occupies exactly half a page. The gentleman in brown-holland casts a look of suspicion at us, and directs a couple of policemen to search us, *registrar* us, as he calls it, which they accordingly do; but nothing that we could dispense with is found on our persons, except the grime upon our hands and faces, and a pearl button, which has strayed during the journey, and somehow found its way into my boot.

Nothing further being required of us for the present, we are conducted into the centre of the jail to an extensive courtyard, where a crowd of prisoners of all shades and castes lie basking in the sun. We are led to one of the galleries which surround the *patio*, our arms are untied, and we are introduced into three different chambers.

The apartment allotted to me is spacious and airy enough, and has a huge barred window that overlooks the main thoroughfare. In these respects, at least, my quarters resemble an ordinary Cuban parlour in a private house. But the only articles of furniture are a couple of hard benches and a straw mattress; and although a Cuban parlour has a barred window, a brick floor, and whitewashed walls, it has also a few cane-bottomed chairs, an elegant mirror, and a gas chandelier.

The prison in which I am confined was originally a convent, and now it is not only devoted to the use of malefactors, but also accommodates mad people, whose shrieks and wild laughter I occasionally hear. From my window I can see into the private houses opposite, where ladies are swaying and fanning themselves in *butacas*, or rocking-chairs, while half a dozen naked white and black children play in an adjacent room. Friends passing along the street recognise me; but I may not converse with them, or the sentry below will inform, and I shall be removed to a more secluded part of the stronghold.

I am not alone. My chamber is occupied by a native Indian, whose origin is distinguishable by his lank, jet-black hair, his gipsy-like complexion, and finely-cut nostrils. He is neither tattooed, nor does he wear feathers, beads or animals' hides; but with the exception of his face and hands (which are very dirty) he has all the appearance of a civilized being.

The Indian has been himself arrested on suspicion, but his trial has been postponed for many weary months, and he is at present quite ignorant of the charge on which he may stand accused. Having no friends to intercede for him, or golden doubloons wherewith to convince the authorities of his innocence, the poor fellow is afraid things will go hard with him.

The Indian is eloquent on the subjects of slavery and Spanish rule, both of which he warmly denounces. He is careful to remind me, that although he speaks the Spanish language, and is governed by Spanish laws, he is no more a Spaniard than is an American an Englishman. There is something in common between these nationalities, he says, whereas between a Cuban and a Spaniard there is a very wide gulf!

My patriotic friend gets so excited over these and other favourite topics that, afraid of the consequences of his conversation, I propose a smoke.

"What!" he exclaims, approaching me in what seems a threatening attitude. "Is it possible that you have any tobacco, and that you are going to smoke some here?"

Lest the Indian should be no smoker himself and dislike the odour of tobacco, I tell him that if he objects, I will postpone my harmless whiff until after captivity.

He does object; but after contemplating my scanty supply of cigarettes as I restore them to my pocket, he observes with a sigh:

"I was once an inveterate smoker!"

"Till you very wisely gave up the vice," I add.

"No!" says he, "I did not give it up. It was my accursed captors who withheld it from me. I have not smoked for many long months, and I would often give 10 years of my life for one little cigarette!"

"Try one of mine," I suggest, extracting the packet again which alas! contains my last four.

"Gracias; no," he replies, "I shall be depriving you, and you will find cigarettes scarce in these quarters!"

"If you are a true Cuban," I observe, "you will remember that it is next to an insult to refuse a man's tobacco. Besides, if you object to my indulging in the luxury upon the plea that the delicious perfume is unendurable in another, both of us will be deprived of the pleasure!"

"You are right," says the Indian, "then I will take just one."

So saying, he accepts the little paper squib which I offer, and carefully divides the contents into two equal parts; explaining, as he does so, how he intends to reserve one half of the tobacco for another occasion.

While thus engaged I am reminded of the awful fact that I have no means of igniting our cigarettes. When I mention this unfortunate circumstance to my companion, he smiles triumphantly, and after placing his ear to the door in melodramatic fashion, proceeds to raise a particular brick in the floor of our apartment under which at least half a dozen matches are concealed.

"These matches," he remarks, "have been treasured in that hole ever since I came to lodge in this jail."

"Have you resided here long?" I inquire.

"It has appeared long to me," he answers, "18 months, more or less; but I have no record of the date."

"You must have found the hours hang heavily on you," I remark, "or, maybe, you have a hobby like the political prisoners one reads of. You have a favorite flower somewhere? Or, perhaps, you are partial to spiders?"

"There are plenty of gigantic spiders here," he replies, "together with centipedes and scorpions; but whenever one of those reptiles crosses my path — I kill it!"

When my fellow-captive learns my nationality, his surprise and pleasure are very great.

"I like the English and Americans," says he, "and I would become one or the other tomorrow, if it were possible."

"You're very kind to express so much esteem for my country-men," I say.

"It is not so much your countrymen," he says, "as your free country with its just and humane laws, which every Cuban admires and covets."

I remind him that, under existing circumstances, I am no better off than he is, though to be sure as a British subject, my consul, who resides in Santiago, will doubtless see me righted.

The Indian is, however, of a different opinion. He assures me that my nationality will avail me nothing if I have no interest with some of the Spanish officials. He gives me instances to prove how it is often out of the power of a consul to assist a compatriot in difficulties.

"Not long since," says my friend, "a marine from your country, being intoxicated, and getting mixed up in a street brawl, was arrested and locked up with a crowd of insubordinate coolies and Spanish deserters. His trial was, as usual, postponed. In the meanwhile, the jail had become overcrowded by the arrival of some wounded soldiers from San Domingo, and your countryman was shipped off with others to another prison at Manzanillo, where he was entered on the list of convicts, and has never been heard of since."

"In this very jail," continues the Indian, "are a couple of American engineers, both of whom stand accused of being concerned in a negro conspiracy, and who have been locked up here for the last six months. They are ignorant of the Spanish language, have mislaid their passports, and have been denied a conference with their consul, who is, of course, unaware of their incarceration."

I make a mental note of this last case, with a view to submit it to the proper authority as soon as I shall be able to do so.

My attention is presently arrested by a sound which reminds me of washing, for in Cuba this operation is usually performed by placing the wet linen on a flat board, and belabouring it with a smooth stone or a heavy roller. My companion smiles when I give him my impression of the familiar sounds, and he tells me that white linen is not the object of the beating, but black limbs! An unruly slave receives his castigation at the jail when it is found inconvenient to perform the operation under his master's roof. No inquiry into the offence is made by the officers of justice; the miscreant is simply ordered 25 or 50 lashes, as the case may be, by his accuser, who acts also as his jury, judge, and occasionally — executioner!

Whilst listening to the unfortunate's groans and appeals for mercy, I watch the proceedings of a chain-gang of labourers, some 20 of whom have left the jail for the purpose of repairing a road in an adjacent street. They are dressed in canvas suits, numbered and lettered on the back, and wear broad-brimmed straw-hats. Each man smokes, and makes a great rattling of his chains as he assists in drawing along the heavy trucks and implements for work. A couple of armed soldiers and three or four prison-warders accompany the gang; the former to keep guard, the latter to superintend the labour. Some of the prisoners sell hats, fans, toys, and other articles of their own manufacture as they go along. One of these industrious gentlemen has entered, chains and all, into a private house opposite, and while he stands bargaining with a highly respectable white, his keeper sits, like Patience, on the door-step smoking a cigar.

I withdraw from the window to meet my jailer, who has brought — not my freedom? no; my food. It is the first meal I have tasted for many long hours, and I am prepared to relish it though it be but a banana and Catalan wine.

These are, however, the least items in the princely fare which the jailer has brought. The whitest of tablecloths is removed from the showiest of trays, and discloses a number of small tureens, in which fish, flesh, and fowl have been prepared in a variety of appetising ways. Besides these are a square cedar-box of guava preserves, a pot of boiling black coffee, a bundle of the best Ti Arriba cigars, and a packet of Astrea cigarettes; all served on the choicest china. This goodly repast cometh from La Señora Mercedes, under whose hospitable roof I have lodged and fed for many months. Doña Mercedes has heard of our captivity, and, without making any enquiry into the nature of our misdemeanour, has instantly despatched one of her black domestics with the best breakfast she can prepare.

The Indian assures me that the admittance into jail of such a collation augurs well. I have doubtless friends who are using their influence with the officials in my behalf, and, in short, he considers my speedy release a certainty.

"Usted gusta?" I invite my companion to share the good things, but he excuses himself by saying that, with his present prospects, he would rather not recall the feeling of a good meal. He, however, partakes of some of my coffee, the odour of which is far too savoury for his self-denial, and helps me with the tobacco.

Breakfast over, I take a siesta on half the furniture, and after a few hours' delicious oblivion am awakened by the jailer, who comes with the welcome news that the court is sitting, and that my presence is required.

"Imprisoned and tried on the same day!" exclaims my Indian friend. "Then," says he, "I may well wish you adieu for ever!"

A Cuban court of justice, broadly described, consists of two old men, a deal table, a bottle of ink, and a boy. One of the elders is the alcalde mayor, an awful being, invested with every kind of administrative power; the other functionary is his *escribano*, or legal man-of-all-work, who dispenses Spanish law upon the principle of "French without a master." He professes to teach prisoners their fate in one easy lesson, without the interposition of either counsel or jury. None but those immediately concerned in the case are admitted into the tribune; so that the prisoner, who is frequently the only party interested, has the court, so to speak, all to himself!

The chamber into which I am ushered on the present occasion has very much the appearance of a schoolroom during the holidays. The walls are whitewashed, and half a dozen short forms lie in disorder about the brick floor. At one end of the apartment is a yellow map of the Antilles; at the other is hung a badly painted oil portrait of her Catholic Majesty Isabella, with a soiled coat-of-arms of Castile above her, and a faded Spanish banner half concealing her royal countenance. Beneath this trophy, on a raised platform, is seated the prison magistrate, or fiscal, as he is called. Before him is a cedar-wood table, with a bottle of ink, a glass of blotting sand and a quire of stamped paper. On his right is an *escribano* and a couple of interpreters, whose knowledge of the English language I afterwards find to be extremely limited. On his left is seated my captive companion Nicasio Rodriguez y Boldu. Everybody present, including a couple of brown-holland policemen at the door, is smoking, which has a sociable air, and inspires me with confidence. Upon my appearance in court everybody rises; the fiscal politely offers me a cigar and a seat on the bench.

As a matter of form — for my Spanish is by no means unintelligible — I am examined through the medium of an interpreter, who makes a terrible hash of my replies. He talks of the "foots of my friend's negro," and the "commandant's, officer's, sergeant's relations," by which I infer that the learned linguist has never overcome the fifth lesson of his Ollendorff. It is accordingly found necessary to conduct the rest of the inquiry in good Castilian.

A great case has been made out against us by the commandant, who represents us in his despatch as spies in league with any quantity of confederates. A pocket-book full of nefarious notes and significant scratches has been found upon me: together with a four-bladed penknife, a metallic corkscrew, a very black lead-pencil, and an ink-eraser! In the commandant's opinion the said notes are, without doubt, private observations on the mysteries of the Morro, and the scratches are nothing more nor less than topographical plans of the fortifications.

Absurd and improbable as the commandant's story may appear, it would have had great weight against us with the fiscal, and considerably protracted the period of our release, were it not for the fact that the fiscal is on intimate terms with my companion's family. This fortunate circumstance, aided by the laudable efforts of my consul, who works wonders with his excellency the governor, enables us to be set at liberty without further delay. There is, however, some difficulty in the case of our black attendant, whom the authorities would still keep in bondage, out of compliment to stern justice; but we intercede for him, and he accompanies us from jail.

Crowds of people await outside and escort us to our studio, where dear old Don Benigno, his amiable señora and family, welcome us with joy. Wherever we go, we are lionised and loaded with congratulations and condolence. A kind of patriotic sentiment is mixed up with the public sympathy; Spanish rule being extremely distasteful to a Cuban, and any opportunity for expressing his disgust of an incompetent ruler being hailed by him with delight. All our Cuban friends — and, to say the truth, many of the Spaniards themselves — are unanimous in their disapproval of the commandant's conduct.

Grover Flint

A Skirmish with The "Gringos," 1896

I joined Lacret on the afternoon of April 4th, just in time to witness a skirmish, and to observe that method of fighting pursued with so much success by the rebels and so little by the Spaniards. Rojas had heard that Lacret was to camp that day with a large force at Pavo Real, an estate in the foothills, midway between Cardenas and Matanzas, and five miles from the shore. The Spanish Colonel Pavia, however, had heard so too, with the result that when we were still three miles from Pavo Real, we heard firing ahead.

We met two peasants on the road, who told us that a big Spanish column had come by rail from Matanzas and had cut across country from Limonar, and were near, very near, — Dios only knew how near. As they spoke, there came a popping like the explosion of a string of fire-crackers, then five crashing volleys rolled through the hills, followed by the sharp rattle of Mausers fired "at will," and our pacifico friends sped on with scarcely an "adios."

A puff of black smoke shot up a mile in front of us, — the black smoke of a peasant's cottage that leaps into the sky with a shower of sparks and dies away quickly. As we looked, another black cloud arose, blowing over the trees this time far to our right. Then we knew that the Spaniards were marching toward the shore, and that Lacret was probably retreating before them. So we turned our horses toward the sea.

It was a pleasant, hilly district, threaded by up and down country lanes, and cut by yellow limestone walls into pastures, canefields, and clumps of scrub forest, — a country for ambuscades and surprises.

Peasants hurried past us, fleeing as from a plague. Old men, women with babies in their arms, and little children tugging at their skirts, ran along, never looking up. Cottages were left vacant; only dogs and hens remained.

At last the crest of a hill opened up a wide view of the ocean. Below us lay rich canefields sweeping to the coastline, with only a fringe of palms and undergrowth between them and the blue sea. Skirting the palms, a long white line of mounted figures moved slowly toward Cardenas; it was Lacret's *impedimenta*, as the unarmed contingent of camp servants and officers' orderlies is called, and a fresh rattle of musketry told that the main force was covering its retreat.

Following a boundary wall through the sloping canefield, we ran into Lacret's rear-guard. Lacret was there himself, surrounded by his staff, peering over the country through his field-glass. A long line of armed men chewing sugarcane and lounging in their saddles were marching off leisurely by twos, after the *impedimenta*, which had already passed. A trooper, shouting "Clear the way," trotted through the group of officers, leading a horse on which were two men, — one holding the other, a negro, on the pommel of his saddle before him. The latter was wounded or dead; for his head hung limp on his breast, and his ragged shirt, open on his black chest, was stained with blood. A dozen stragglers came galloping up, leaning on their horses' necks, and leaped or scrambled through gaps in the boundary wall. One of them, a lieutenant distinguished only by a star on his crossbelt, rode up to Lacret. "They kept coming, and we were out of ammunition," he said.

Back in the olive angle, where the canes and palm shadows met, a gray speck appeared, enlarging swiftly and extending toward us.

Lacret turned in his saddle. "Captain Camaguey," he said, "make another ambuscade with 20 men behind this wall." Then he rode on, followed by the staff.

As we tagged on after him, a young officer, Duque Estrada, told me the story of the fight. "At noon," he said, "we were camped on the hill called Pavo Real, when scouts galloped in with news that Pavia was near, marching from Limonar, with a full column of cavalry and infantry, — perhaps 1,500 men. It was almost a surprise; for we did not expect troops from that direction. We had scarcely time to mount and form when they came in sight, deploying over the hillsides and fields to the west in an effort to surround us. The general sent out two parties, 40 each, of armed men, who took strong positions behind walls and thickets, leaving between them a free road toward the coast, through which our unarmed men rode in safety. Lacret's *escolta* — or bodyguard — held the hill, and as soon as the *impedimenta* were out of the way we followed them, dropping small bunches of men behind to ambuscade the enemy from every wooded hill or limestone wall that could furnish a cover. You can see by the smoke that they are burning all the peasants' houses we have passed, — beginning with the one at Pavo Real. They are brave today," — he said *bravo*, which means at once, angry, persistent, valorous, aggressive — "and have kept after us, although we have left five *ambuscades* and they must have lost quite a few men already."

Two scouts galloped suddenly from a *guarda-raya* of the canefield through which my little party had just passed. "The gringos!" they shouted; "the cavalry are coming. Many, many of them! They are coming through the cane to head us off!" Over the crest of the hill a dark moving something appeared, approaching diagonally. Pavia's mind had expanded with a stratagem, and things looked serious.

Lacret turned back to where Camaguey was placing his handful, of men for the sixth ambuscade. "Give them a *candela*," he said.

A negro, without dismounting, cut a bunch of palm leaves by the roadside, twisted them together into a torch, and lighted it, galloping along by the side of our retreating line of men. He leaned low from his saddle, switching the sputtering torch under the skirts of the cane shoots; another negro dismounted, climbed over the wall with a bunch of matches, and fanning vigorously with his hat, kindled a fire on the other side.

A strong breeze was blowing from the sea; the canes were ablaze with frightful heat in a moment, and the heavy smoke and flame were swept in the face of the Spanish cavalry. We had nothing more to fear from that quarter.

A popping from Camaguey's men joined the crackling of burning cane. The gray line of Spaniards was now within easy range, and the sharp pah! pah! pah! of Mausers, with a psit! of an occasional bullet, lower aimed than the others, came in return.

The Spaniards advanced a little and drew up to shoot again.

Lacret, sitting on his horse by the wall, watched the flames spreading before the wind. He was very conspicuous, wearing a tall Mexican hat, and you could hear shouts of "Tira al sombrero alto" (Shoot at the tall hat). Then we left Camaguey and rode after the main force. That was the last ambuscade of the day.

It was now four o'clock in the afternoon. The Spaniards sent half a dozen volleys in our direction, and fell back toward Pavo Real. Our column took to the forest-clad hummocks at the base of the peninsula Hicacos, and as we looked back, the whole country seemed ablaze. Four miles of sugarcane skirting the shore was afire, and back among the hills of Pavo Real rose the blacker smoke of burning cottages.

This skirmish cost Lacret two out of 200 *armados*, one of whom was buried, when the troops ceased to pursue, among the scrub trees of the peninsula. The other received a fatal wound from a stray shot at very long range, perhaps a mile, and after his troop was under cover. A nickel-covered Mauser bullet pierced the small of his back, passed through the thumb of his bridle hand, and buried itself in the pommel of his saddle.

We camped that night in the overseer's cottage on a sugar estate, three miles out of Cardenas, and as I sat at supper with Lacret, scouts reported the enemy's position in the immediate neighborhood. Pavia had made camp in a sugar-house five miles away, near Pavo Real. Three miles to the south of us, camping on another large plantation, was a Spanish column of 800 men which had marched that afternoon from Cardenas. To the northeast, at scarcely a greater distance, lay

Cardenas with its garrison of regulars and volunteers. It was fair to suppose that with reasonable activity, Spanish scouting parties might locate us during the night and have every lane and trail about us ambuscaded by morning.

I asked Lacret if we were not in a bit of a hole, and my question surprised him.

"They will not know where we are," he said, "until they hear it from peasants tomorrow. They never dare to send out scouts: if they did, I should capture them at once. They only move about the country in heavy columns, and I can skirmish with them or evade them as I like. By tomorrow they will know that we have been here and they will march here on principle; but by sunrise I shall be gone, and they will not know where I am, excepting by accident, until 24 hours later." I found that Lacret was not guilty of exaggeration.

Meanwhile the dying man was given a room to himself, and the surgeon tried to do something for him. At sundown his wound began to pain him, and his groans, "Ay, Dios mio! Ay, Dios mio!" broke the stillness of the night until death came early the next morning.

Irene A. Wright

Cuban Home Life, 1910

This household, on whose daily life we have looked down for four years, has afforded me a better insight into the intimate existence of city-dwelling Cubans of the middle class than I could otherwise have obtained except through the ordeal of actually sharing it. The house itself in which we three families live together is not without interest to visitors. It is in shape a hollow square, fitted tight into a solid block. It stands on a narrow downtown street in Havana, presenting a façade unadorned save by a wooden door, wide and high as a commodious barn's, of some dark color, in which heads of great nails, or imitation heads, show through the paint; and two windows, tall and narrow, barred like those of a county jail, shutters of which (there is no glass) remain turned until late in the afternoon, to keep out as far as possible dust, the glare of the sun on the yellow walls of the Supreme Court opposite, and especially the nerve-wracking, ceaseless noise of cars, carts, automobiles, and street vendors, as, chanting, honking, rumbling, and clanging, they collaborate to maintain pandemonium. The street wall of the house is smoothly plastered and tinted a fading pale green. Passing conveyances have splashed it with mud. There is, before it, no sidewalk at all, but a narrow coping of stone. Electric cars whiz so close that passengers can, and do, touch its window bars by half-extending their arms. On both sides of our house are others somewhat similar in externals; one is a modern two-story double apartment, erected since we have been here, to rent, and the other is a tenement which teems with mulattoes and blacks. In the block below us are the Department of Public Instruction and the National Library; opposite the immense structure which shelters these and other government offices is a building which used to be the Court of First Instance, but now rents by the room to individuals, — among them a "hair-dresser" whose sign appears, I notice, at irregular intervals and in unusual business hours: sometimes at night a broad stream of brilliant light falls from her open door across the street outside, and passers-by, glancing in, see a bed with a Spanish lace spread, decorated with bow-knots of scarlet ribbon.

One raps on our door with a small iron knocker, entirely uninteresting in age and design, and in the great door a small door opens cautiously; one is admitted grudgingly. Nothing small annoys me more than the way they open doors in Cuba, peer forth through the crack, or a peephole especially cut for the purpose, demand one's business as they would a password, leave one standing outside while they close the door and retreat to consult, finally permitting one, possibly, to squeeze through. Experience has, to quote a sentence I read yesterday, "thrown a permanent scare into the Cuban soul." At their thresholds they show it. I long to leap through crying "Boo!"

Admitted into our house, one finds himself in a wide entry. From the stone flagging of the slanting floor to the close-raftered ceiling stretch about 25 feet of whitewashed wall. This entry is large enough to accommodate a carriage, if there were one; it was intended for that purpose. Under the backstairs there is room for a horse, but it is used instead to store old furniture. At the end of the entry, opposite the street door, there is a grille which may be locked or made to swing open hospitably in halves. Passing through one arrives in the dining room, which is also the living room of the "family downstairs."

Nothing could be more instructive than this dining room. There is a central table of considerable extension, for the family which gathers about it is numerous. It is covered, between meals, with a cloth of imitation tapestry. There is a spidery black hatrack with a broken glass in it. Opposite, an old-fashioned, high sideboard of cheap yellow wood; on it stand crystal and blue glass dishes, cups, tumblers, crumpled napkins, playthings, and schoolbooks. In the corner is a filter. On the wall, an octagonal clock with a time-yellowed face. Under it, a row of rocking-chairs.

Up one wall of the dining room rises a narrow wooden stairway to the floor above, where "the Americans" dwell, "on the roof" and isolated. They pay about two *centenes* a month, in their rent, for the exclusive privilege of their quarters. No one has a right to ascend those stairs without their implied permission, nor pass the door at the turn, which may be locked, without knocking. The American family in the tenement adjoining is not so fortunate, for all the inmates of that house have the run of the stairs there, and washerwomen pass back and forth through their hallway with clothes.

Off the dining room, back in the direction of the street, downstairs in our house, is the parlor, reached by way of an immense door. This room is usually half darkened. Its walls are like those of the entry, high and white; they give a barren, empty aspect, and dwarf the furniture, which seems scant. There is a piano in a black case; it is thin-toned and out of tune. There are chairs of several woods and as many patterns; they know their places and keep them. There is a center table cluttered with worthless trinkets, — tiny animals in bisque, artificial flowers, and porcelain figurettes. The whole place smells damp and musty.

Another door from the dining room leads into the daughters' bedroom, of which I have noticed only a high wardrobe with a long mirror in which I remember seeing the girls pleasantly reflected as they turned and twisted before it, one dressed in pink and the other in blue, arraying themselves for their first ball. Adjoining theirs is the mother's bedroom, which has a door and a barred window on the *patio*. Here is a wide, four-post bed, wardrobes, and a washstand.

The *patio* is a square, stone-paved open court, into which the dining room, too, has a pair of doors. The walls about it are painted an atrocious blue. There are palms and foliage plants in tubs and tins that match the walls in color. From their roof neighbors in the tenement next door can look into the *patio;* their variegated children lean sometimes along the top of its wall and comment upon whatever may be transpiring below. The family on the second floor of the apartment house on the other side from their roof can catch glimpses of anything of interest going on, and their children cast pebbles and small sticks down. These rattle cheerily on the tin roof of the lean-to in the *patio* which is the bathroom. It shelters a big tub of tile, once white, set into cement. Here are stored wash-tubs, foot-tubs, wash-pans, dirty clothes, in various degrees of uncleanliness and corrosion. Havana has not yet a sewer system. I presume, however, because we are near the sea, that there is a connection between our plumbing and some drainpipe, rather than a cesspool under the court.

At the back of the house, from wall to wall, is the kitchen, — roomy enough (most kitchens in new houses are very small), littered and smoky where, over charcoal on braziers, the cook prepares rare dishes: we perceive odors of scorched milk, garlic, saffron, and frying oil. Above the kitchen are two dark, close rooms reached by back-stairs, where dwells "the woman in the rear."

There are, then, in all the house downstairs, no windows to the street save the two in the parlor. There is no yard, either front or back: the *patio* is the substitute, and the flat roof, which, in this parti-cular instance, we tenants of the upper floor monopolize. There is not, in all the establishment, a single article or incident of comfort. There is no way to warm any part of the house, nor, fortunately, is it ever really necessary. The light is gas, in unprotected jets that flare. Hot water *non est,* except as it boils from the faucet on summer days when the sun has been at the pipes for a few moments, undisturbed. There is not, if one excepts the growing plants which flower now and then in defiance of neglect, one item of beauty, — not a picture, not a book excepting text-books from school. It is, I am confident, a fairly typical home of city Cubans of limited means.

If this family had money, the house would change in some res-pects. The flooring of the downstairs rooms, instead of tiles, would be marble blocks. The walls of the rooms would remain high, but the rafters above might disappear under a stucco ceiling and the whole color of the chambers change from a dingy white to delicate tones of cream, blue, or pink. The furniture would come in "sets;" it would lose, however, none of the prim orderliness of its arrangement. Pictures in obtrusively ornate gilt frames would appear upon the walls. Under a gardener's care the *patio* would become a beautiful formal garden instead of a hodgepodge of whatever happens to live. The plumbing would improve in externals, but not at all in essentials. The kitchen would hardly gain. There would, in summary, remain much of the roominess or emptiness, much of the free air and available sunlight, which, once one is accustomed to them, make American houses seem close, dark, and suffocating; there would also remain much of the bad taste (it runs to "tidies," paper flowers, and knicknacks) which is scarce in our house because its residents cannot afford it, but loads the wobbly center tables and corner whatnots of wealthy Cubans with porcelain pigs, bisque doll babies, china dogs, and seashells.

The mother of "the family downstairs" and her daughters despise work, — more, I am convinced, from a notion that it is unbecoming to a lady, than from laziness. Although, from an American standpoint, they can very ill afford it, they not only tolerate, but pay a little money to soiled and unskilled serving people no really thrifty housewife could be hired to have about. There are usually three servants: a slattern cook, a nursemaid of little better appearance, and a Spanish boy recently passed through the Immigrant Camp at Triscornia.

The cook "sleeps out." She (once it was a decrepit negro man) puts in an appearance some time after seven o'clock with a flat, round basket containing materials for the day's meals, — diminutive tomatoes, thick-skinned red or green plantains, *boniatos,* which are insipid sweet potatoes, beans, in a small brown paper parcel with the corners twisted to make it serve as a bag, rice, a fish, or a little meat. She has paid one, two, three, and four cents for each article — much more for the fish or meat — out of a *per diem* allowance made her, from which, in addition to a low wage, she collects her percentage of profit. If the allowance is small, the quality of what she buys is frequently not of the best. Now "the family downstairs" could not permit any member, were any so strenuously inclined, to go into the reeking market in person to haggle with recalcitrant Spanish stall keepers for tomatoes of respectable size, meat of an edible cut, or eggs "of the country," not "of the north," for to do that is to lose caste, as have "the Americans of the upstairs," who as they climb homewards with the best there is, in paper bags, — choice cuts of fillet, treasures of young beets, green peas not oiled, and unspotted melons, — return the contemptuous glances bestowed by "the family downstairs" with an equally contemptuous gaze of comment on the quality and preparation of the food their cook dishes up.

The cook does not serve the first meal. About four o'clock in the morning the milkman with thunderous rap, repeated like a bombardment, succeeds eventually in rousing the Spanish boy (who sleeps, half clad, on a cot in the entry by the door), to force into his groping hand a pewter can of milk. This the nursemaid heats over an alcohol lamp, and at intervals, as they appear, the members of the family take their morning "coffee with milk." Sometimes they gather, uncombed and half dressed, about the table from which the tapestry cloth has been jerked; it lies carelessly thrown across a chair close by, while they eat off the oilcloth, slopped with milk and water and strewn with bread, which in broken pieces the serving boy hands out from the side-board drawer. "Breakfast" occurs at about eleven, and dinner at about seven at night.

Formerly the two older girls used to attend a convent school near by. Their mother saw them to the street door, and, together, they were permitted to walk unattended the two blocks necessary. Meanwhile, at home, the littlest girl sang "b—a, ba!" for hour after hour from her primer, on the supposition that she, also, was learning. She "ba—ed" her way into a neat blue uniform of her own finally, and was duly admitted to attendance at the same school. Jesusito, the baby, then quarreled with his fat black nurse unhectored, ordered his *mamaita* about like a young dictator, fondled the cat (taboo pet of the Americans above), smiled shyly at them, and shook, not "daydays" as American babies do, but innumerable "goo-byes" from among the palms. The mother seemed always busy; sometimes she sewed. Her shrill, cutting voice kept up a constant rasping comment on the day's progress. Late in the afternoons, when school was out, she gathered her girls about her, in the rocking-chairs under the clock. Perhaps they sewed, or the more accomplished read in English, chanting the words in a strained high key, without proper accent, in most unnatural manner. The baby played with his horse on wheels. The servants stole a moment to themselves. The Americans from above, noting the family group and its contentment, nodded to each other in approval. "The woman in the rear," smoking in her kitchen window, looked on. Her only son is grown.

We can always tell when *el señor* — father of "the family down-stairs" — is expected home, to visit or to stay as long as he can, in the "dead season." He is a *colono* on a big sugar plantation in Santa Clara, — that is, he grows cane on shares. For two or three days prior to his arrival there is uproar below. The servants are harried hither and yon by orders given in conflict by everybody at once in piercing voice. The Spanish boy pours water by the bucketful on all the floors; he sweeps the flags and mops the tiles. He dusts the walls with a rag on a long bamboo. He brings forth palms from the *patio*, and stands them here and there. The daughters tie tissue paper around their tubs and tins, with ribbon. The mother dons a lavender wrapper with a great bow to match on her breast. She combs her thick black hair beautifully, and the touch of white across her temple (which distracts her and occasions inquiry into reliable dyes) gives her an air of distinction; she is nearer a beauty than either of her girls. A knock, — the door is opened to a crack, and then flung wide. "Jesusito!" we hear the sisters scream to the baby at his play, "Papa has come! He's come!" They carry his boy to his arms. They eddy about him in an animated whirl, seizing his satchel, his hat; patting his hair, his hands; hugging him ecstatically, and talking loudly all together. Through the discord his voice sounds like a bass viola.

That night's dinner is a state occasion. They put a tiny plant, tied up with tissue paper and ribbon like the rest, in the middle of the table. The Spanish boy laughs as he serves; he spills the soup and wipes his hand on the seat of his trousers before handing up "a bread" from the basket at the end of the table. The uncorseted nurse behind the baby's chair jiggles like jelly as she laughs to make the baby crow louder. All lean on their elbows and ply knife, fork, and spoon industriously and indiscriminately, turning at intervals open, half-filled mouths to the father as, from the place of honor, he tells them incidents of his life "up country." If napkins slip to the floor, they use the hanging edge of the tablecloth. It is the mother herself who brings forward from the kitchen a custard for dessert in making which she spent half a day. Over the coffee they linger long. When, finally, they arise, the table cover is wrinkled and damp and soiled at the edges and in spots everywhere; the setting is awry, and bread and crumbs and bones and peelings litter it from end to end.

That evening they sit in a row in the chairs under the clock, father and mother side by side and hand in hand. The girls crowd close about him, the littlest at his knee. The baby climbs into her lap, and sleeps.

When in time *el señor* returns, as he must, to the sugar estate, a renewal of commotion marks the day of his departure. Again the servants are hustled about and sharp staccato shrieks arise from the *patio*. I have never heard voices that reminded me so strongly of an orchestra tuning up. The girls bring their father's clothing. The mother packs his satchel, with pink and blue shirts and socks and linen suits. They accompany him to the train, and, when they get back from the station, sit silently in a row in the selfsame chairs under the noisy clock. The tissue paper disappears from the tubs; they go back to the *patio*. The purple wrapper is hung away. The tablecloth writhes in new wrinkles over the board. I have seen the Spanish boy seize it at both ends, roll it into a bundle, — crumbs, bones, peelings, and all, — and thrust it, unshaken and unfolded, into the sideboard drawer along with the accumulating crusts of stale bread. The current of small events resumes its usual flow. From the *altos* the Americans look down, in superiority, over late risings, burnt milk breakfasts, and a scant wash half clean, listlessly wrung from a shallow pan. From the *patio* those below look up, with curled lips, as the Americans, with dripping mop, wipe up their own floors, cook their own meals, wash their own dishes, only to sally forth later unashamed, and wearing hats. Ah, those hats are our revenge, obtained at intervals. Having bought a new one, we pay cash and order it delivered. We know that the uniformed boy makes a great clatter on the front door, that he pushes the tremendous box in before him, and follows it importantly, that he sets it carefully upon our stairs, according to instructions, and retires, leaving all who are in the vicinity to study, in what mood they will, the French title upon that box. Our hats hail from Obispo, — and theirs from Galiano or San Rafael streets. We reflect upon that detail, and are comforted as we endure their contumely amid our homely tasks. "The woman in the rear," smoking in her kitchen window, — she has no hat at all.

Each year at about Christmas time, or after carnival, perhaps, "the family downstairs" goes into the country to spend the rest of "the grinding season" with *el señor* on his *colonia*. Last June, when they came home, we recognized that an important event had occurred meanwhile. The girls had become young ladies: their hair was piled high, their dresses were made long, a touch of rouge illumined their cheeks, and there was powder upon their noses. No more blue, convent uniforms for them, — the littlest was alone in that glory. Then, indeed, there was a how-de-do. The house was whitewashed inside and painted outside. The plant tubs and tins in the *patio* were daubed anew with cerulean. The best palms took permanent place in the corners, and tissue paper and ribbons embellished them even in the father's absence. Then a governess came of mornings: she taught French, I think, as well as English, music (chopsticks were abandoned and the eldest mastered a waltz), and sewing. I have seen both girls stretched almost full length across the table, poring together over *Modes de Paris* before proceeding to copy "the latest" as best they were able, in 30-cent figured lawn, bought in some one of numerous shopping expeditions to "The Enchantment," "The Great House," or "Philosophy." To their credit be it said they did attain effect; their gowns were sometimes minus buttons and exhibited rows of pins down the back, but few American girls with as scant training and as little to do with, could compass the appearance these girls made, seen from a distance. In the afternoon they posed at their street windows, their mother rocking in her chair just behind them, or they walked out with her. The mother, too, had a new gown, a cheap little imitation of an American tailor-made; unlike most chaperones who tag the eligibles, she was in her neat and attractive self a recommendation of her girls. Sometimes they went to the theater, airing light and filmy scarfs; they returned home toward midnight, accompanied by whatever other family had invited them, and at the clatter of tongues as they bade mutual good nights the Americans upstairs woke and turned impatiently in bed. Or there was company in the evening; until midnight then we were tormented with loud laughter and many voices in dissonant chorus, among which we could now and then distinguish the uncertain tenor of some young man we knew was sitting on the edge of his chair cooling himself rapidly with a small black fan, which he replaced at intervals in his waistcoat pocket. On this, too, "the woman in the rear," smoking in her kitchen window, looked down interestedly. Her son is only a mechanic.

During the family's absence in the country each season, caretakers have been installed. Once it was a round, kind woman and her come-

ly daughter, to court whom a policeman called. He was rather handsome in his blue uniform, and they held forth in the chairs under
the clock, openly fondling each other. The mother bent low over the
dining table, spelling out the Associated Press telegrams in the *Diario
de la Marina*. I ventured to compliment her once on her prospective
son-in-law. She spoke disrespectfully of him: he had been courting
nine years, and now earned only 30 dollars a month, on which he
and his sweetheart agreed that they dared not marry. Yet they could
not break off the match, or the girl would be ruined, so carping is
custom here. Already her sweet face had taken on a shade of tragedy.

This year, however, when the family went they left in charge
"the woman in the rear." Prior to that time she had lived in two
rooms and a stair landing, at the back of the house above their
kitchen. These rooms have two windows, barred, overlooking the
patio, and a door opening on the back roof, to half of which only are
we "Americans of the upstairs" entitled.

Before she occupied them, these rooms were filled with two very
old ladies, one of whom was bedridden, their niece, Doña Maria,
who sewed for a pittance, her son, German, a boy such as God sends
infrequently, and the bent old black hag who served them to the
very ending of her strength. The negress delivered *cantina* dinners
for a restaurant by day, for what few pennies it paid, and at night
she fished in the garbage for what she might find. Between times
she cooked and washed and waited upon her mistresses. She was
the last faithful slave of their retinue. She slept in one room; they,
Doña Maria and the child, slept in the other, — the sick woman in a
heavily curtained unaired bed, and the rest on cots, with the windows
and doors all closed. Fortunately, the walls do not quite touch the
roof, and under the eaves there is a ventilation they could not stop
up. In this bedroom was an altar, gaudily trimmed, before which
they burned an uninterrupted lamp of oil. The negress died, and
two strange women of her own race, as silent and as old, came in a
carriage and laid her out; they came again and carried her away,
having begged permission to take her down our stairs, which have
only one turn. Later still, the sick one of the two old white women
died and was buried; German, the child, pitiful and lonely in his
black, rode after her body in a carriage, her only mourner. The
survivors prepared then to move away, as is the custom when death
occurs. The remaining old lady brought us a gift of two china cups

with her initials burned in, in gold, part, evidently, of an especially made imported set. We urged her to save them for German when he should be grown. She said she had a cupboardful beside. Doña Maria gave us a glass butter plate such as one could buy for five cents in a department store; and so they passed out of our lives, struggling on in theirs. We saw them go with keen regret, for these were gentlefolk.

When first we spied her face at the window "the woman in the rear" looked very dark-complexioned to us. We don't see that now, since we know her. Her husband is an artisan, — a plumber and boilermaker, machinist and engineer, combined, as nearly as I am able to discover. He is about 60 years of age, and won't, so his wife says, admit it. Certainly he does not look it, though he is gaunt and tall and grizzled. He wears the expression of an exceedingly good-natured Russian hound. She is 35. Their only son, an artisan like his father, is about 20, I suppose. When first they moved in, these three kept close to their quarters and surveyed us through the bars. I do not recall how the almost intimate acquaintance between us first began; perhaps it was spontaneous, for certainly we have much in common with these Cubans. They are country people from Pinar, and typical, I take it, not of any class in any city, but of the middle class of a small town.

The altar where the former tenants enshrined their Virgin has become a sideboard. There is not a sacred picture, a holy lamp, or a scapular to be found on the premises. Perfect cleanliness prevails. There is a red cloth on the dining table in the largest room. There are a few chromos hung around. There is a swinging lamp with a red shade, and in the evenings they light it and sit under it in rocking-chairs, all three smoking together. In the bedroom there is a four-poster, and the counterpane and pillow slips are clean; they are hand-embroidered and trimmed with lace Doña Pilar crochets. One night the rats ran through, and bit the mother's ankle as she slept. They nibbled the finger tips of the boy, asleep on his cot in the middle room; he had been eating cheese the night before. After that Doña Pilar gave the American's cat the run of her rooms; in the first three days she was installed below as caretaker she caught 19 rats in a trap and drowned them in a washtub.

By the door to the back *azotea* (roof) are Doña Pilar's flowering plants in rusting pots. There is no paint here, but there is more bloom than all the *patio* below can show. The son fashioned a tiny watering pot from a condensed milk can, for his mother to sprinkle her garden, and many are the mornings we have seen him out, bending over her as she showed him one by one the new blossoms as they burst open to the day.

Anaïs Nin

From The Early Diary, 1922

Havana, 1922

October 9

...I have seen the city from the lowest to the highest houses. I have become familiar with its strange little houses painted white and yellow and pale blue and rose; have distinguished a quaint charm in a mass of bizarre coloring, in the narrow streets. One passes over the dirt and the laziness and the vivid, vulgar ornamentations and the primitive, barbaric traits that cannot be denied, and finds much that appeals in its inhabitants. The poor are desperately poor; the rich are ostentatiously rich, but one feels in sympathy with both. Whatever repels is redeemed by much that is touching.

Havana strikes me as a city of extremes, of contrasts, or it may only seem so because it is comparatively small. It seems all to be condensed in a handful, so to speak, and can be so easily observed...

November 9

...Havana, en masse, vaguely stirs in one memories of pictures of ancient Moorish cities — cream-white stone houses, flat-roofed, with arched doorways, columns and balconies, all linked, following the fantastic curves of narrow, irregular streets. Or it rouses faint recollections of old Spain, and vestiges of Spanish dominion are distinguishable everywhere, in the homes of the middle class, with their plaster-walled, high-roofed, stone-floored rooms; in the Cubans' dress, taste, and customs.

Tradition hangs about the quaint furniture, and nothing within the commonplace home is either modern or even moderately up to date. And tradition walks about the streets, too, and one is strongly tempted to plead thus: for less tradition and more cleanliness!

Shops, cafés, etc. open out upon the streets. Misery is more apparent since one can see into the inmost heart of the houses through wide windows and doors flung open — across rooms to the very backyard. A habit of inordinate hospitality fostered by the climatical conditions and atmospheric pressure!

Poverty stands fully revealed, naked, a striking, repulsive sight to a stranger until all feeling of condemnation melts into an all-absorbing compassion.

In the walk of the people about the streets is reflected a peculiar indolence. It is a slow, dragging step, a deliberate, swinging movement, a gliding, serpentlike motion, something speaking indefinably of that characteristic laziness of the tropics and a something else which might be called a state of mental apathy, a universal malady of Havana, at least to my mind. Mental idleness, vacuity, are what I read in most passing faces. Eyes seeming to wander forever, alighting on everything but carrying no thoughts to the mind, eyes devoid of vision, gleaming alone when the senses are pleased... All this with a few exceptions, but it strikes one as universal in comparison with the expressions on the faces of any other crowd or mere passers-by of other cities.

Traces of religious bigotry — a deep-seated ignorance and superstitious slavery to custom — the total absence of individual will, intelligence, understanding, a faith of childish simplicity, all these are still found in some women here. And in most cases she does not even fulfill the demands of beauty for she lacks grace and charm and culture. Vanity is her all-absorbing passion and only interest, and whatever else conforms with the character of the doll that she is. If she is sweet and submissive, it is the submission of unconscious inferiority. All this, with exceptions and taking into consideration that the younger girls, educated abroad, are returning with knowledge and ideals, so that for Havana, as for every city, one can count on the gradual influence of progress...

November [?]
Notes on a Visit to the Convent of Santa Clara
Through a curious architecture, twisted to meet the need of aggrandizement, a whole world lay enclosed within the high, forbidding outer wall, a world of many houses linked to one another by passageways and little wooden bridges, forming spaces and courts in so immense and confused a plan that no clear conception of it could be gained in a short visit.

Quaint and unforgettable details could be gathered on the way, suggesting bygone centuries — old lanterns; arched colonnades; wide windows, heavily barred with iron, opening upon the street; heavy, imposing doors creaking on their ancient, rusty hinges or locked by ancient, rusty locks; and every stone, every step, old, worn, and yellow.

It was sad to have its historical sacredness thus violated by the intrusion of unfeeling strangers. To the poet or the dreamer the place was filled with traces that he could recognize and by which he could reconstruct the broken web of many human documents.

One could imagine the old garden in the tender sunlight, calm, serene, and nuns gliding about, softly murmuring their beads; or moving across the frail wooden bridges and bending over the wooden banister... shadows crowding in one's mind, fantastic characters of one's own making, moving, giving a semblance of life... praying, laboring, and then at night perhaps retiring into their bare, cold cells to sleep on their beds of board. And the candlelight perhaps trembling in the still night and throwing the shadows of their window bars upon the stone floor — the symbol of their voluntary exile and imprisonment.

Days later
Since then I have heard many stories about the old convent which have supplied the last touch of reality to my fantastic imaginings —

stories of folded love notes found in the crevice of a door, of drawers in the kitchen wall through which the nuns did their marketing, of secret tunnels under the chapel leading out into the city for the escape of the nuns at the time when they lived in constant fear of the pirates and of pillages (to protect their treasures, the walls were built so high and so forbidding and the windows barred and the doors massive, strongly locked), of the well in the center of the court, dating back as far as 400 years, and of the "poseta," or kind of public bath.

Some are in possession of documents and diaries in the handwriting of the nuns themselves, strange, romantic stories of girls seeking refuge in religion, the seclusion of the cloister against the cruelty of parents forcing them to marry against their inclination; stories probably of unrequited love, of disappointments, of separations by violence or misunderstanding — of all the causes, in short, which can turn a creature against the world and move her to total renunciation of it. It is curious to notice how few are the people who have faith in the vocation — in a pure, religious spirit, in a truly pious inspiration...

T. Phillip Terry

Terry's Guide to Cuba, 1929

The present-day Cuban

The present-day Cuban is rapidly becoming Americanized *(ameri-canizado)*. Thousands act, think, talk, and look like Americans; wear American clothes, ride in American autos; use American furniture and machinery; oftentimes send their children to American colleges; live for a time in the States themselves or expect to, and eat much American food. A great and growing army of them speak English with a fluency that arouses the envy of the linguistically limited northerner who tries to master the sonorous Spanish. Unlike many other Latins their ideals are American and it is noteworthy that when they speak English they usually omit the expressive gesticulations apparently inseparable from Castilian speech. The sensational news-papers growl at American and British possession of many of the sugar-estates of the island; the grafting politician enthusiastically curses the American and Canadian bankers who keep the country on a safe financial keel but keep just as vigilant an eye on interest collections; and rattle-pated wags deplore every influence from the North. But the honest, thoughtful, grateful Cuban of the old régime, with a memory for past favors says: "The United States has been a Godsend to Cuba, a generous fountain whence Cuba has drawn unthinkable benefits. What would have become of Cuba had the priceless friendship of the U.S. been withheld? To such sincere Cubans (of which there are many) the shadow of the colossus of the North looming above the horizon spells the safety that the shallow water does to the little fish pursued by the big shark. Tio Sam is regarded as the champion of the rights of the smaller republics; he has been tried in the fire of adversity and has been found helpful and good. The Cuban conviction that Uncle Sam doesn't covet his territory and will never be a menace to him is perhaps unique in Spanish America.

Intercourse with the people

The wary Anglo-Saxon familiar with Spanish American characteristics is apt not to place too much dependence on the grandiloquent phraseology and the exaggerated courtesy of certain natives he meets. He knows that to be *simpatico* (amiable) at any cost usually is their aim, and that this sometimes leads them into making promises they have no intention of abiding by. It is generally with this idea in the back of his mind that the linguistically economical and reserved northerner regards the Cuban. But gradually this is dislodged and he comes to believe him sincere. In traveling about the country, the visitor learns that politeness, helpfulness, and consideration are not confined to any special class. Usually the most humble workers, black, white, or brown are as courteous as the highest. An altruistic helpfulness for which no financial gain is expected is one of the most pleasing of the national characteristics.

An admirable attitude for a stranger to adopt in a foreign country is that of an uncritical and amiable observer. To visit a foreign land with preconceived notions tinged with prejudice is to detract from one's enjoyment of it. The judicious person refrains from criticizing local customs, rarely judges nations by individuals, and usually keeps in mind the old truism that it is useless to go to Rome if you quarrel with the Pope. Resolute good-humored credulity in the matter of church miracles, island legends, anecdotes of great men, and war-like valor is a valuable asset. It costs nothing to believe the stories one hears, and oftentimes the deceit is pleasant. A method for selecting one's ancestors has not yet been devised, and persons who are discourteous to colored people because they are colored, and who derive pleasure from calling them black-and-tans, oftentimes unwittingly wound kind and generous hearts. One never gains by seeking motes in bright eyes.

The polite, tolerant visitor to Cuba will get real enjoyment out of his sojourn if he radiates consideration and views the island and its people *en color de rosa*. It is unjust to measure their institutions by American standards for Cuba is a young country and the people have not yet had time to polish their civilization as they propose to. By eschewing politics (which the foreigner cannot understand) and religion (which is always a debatable subject), and by conforming as nearly as possible to established customs, the visitor will gain the esteem of those whose opinion he may well value. The traveler should always remember that many Cubans speak or understand English, and that in Cuba as elsewhere the walls have ears. Likewise that certain natives, without a clear understanding of its value, resent the Platt Amendment, and do not like to speak of it. Sometimes when the American refers to it the polite native will say: *no toquemos esa cuerda,* let's not touch on that chord…

Americans in Cuba

Americans in Cuba are cautioned against the (usually soused) sailors who, with no passion for clean linen or a shave, accost them and spin disconnected yarns about having been left in a strange land by their ships, etc. etc. Also against the well-dressed panhandler who opens the interview by calling one "friend" or "brother," asks the way to this or that place; inquires if he likes "this rotten country" and if he thinks it is "as good as the little old U.S.," then mentions his inability to get a decent job and winds up by "touching" him for whatever he can get. If the tourist has a lady with him the stranded countryman usually opens up in this wise: "Pardon me, brother, but I see you have a lady with you, and I want to ask her if she knows the street number of such and such store." The way being paved, a tragic picture of a gentleman in a heartless foreign city is painted, and an effort made to enlist the woman's sympathies. Generous Cubans are often the victims of these wiles, and perchance mindful of favors received in the U.S., allow themselves to receive the *sablazo* (sabre-thrust). What these professionals want is not food but jackrabbit whiskey, good Bacardi, or the excellent cigarettes for which Cuba is famous. In its desire to be friendly to strangers the Cuban government and the police are more lenient with this beach-combing class than it deserves. Attracted by booze, in winter they emulate the vagrant wild-fowl and flock to Cuba in appreciable num-bers. By refusing to support them in idleness the tourist will earn the thanks of govt. and all industrious folks.

The visitor is particularly cautioned against the rapidly increasing crop of child beggars. Knowing the American to be generously in-clined, low class children ask strangers on the street to "gimme one cent" and usually have their ambition gratified. Better-bred children whose parents would be deeply mortified if they knew of it, copy this custom and frequently accost tourists. They buy candy with the money, and by acceding to their requests the stranger runs the risk of making professional beggars out of children while laying an added burden on the state...

The aftermath of the American intervention

The aftermath of the American Intervention was of transcendental importance to Cuba, for with the army of occupation, and later, came certain shrewd men who, charmed by the island and its people, cast their lot with them, and by so doing influenced Cuban progress in an extraordinary way. The majority of educated Cubans adopted the professions of politics, law, medicine, journalism, literature, teaching, engineering and whatnot. With the intellectuals, of which there are many, they gave but scant thought to the vast undeveloped resources of the island; perchance because for many years the plant-ations, shops and business in general had been conducted chiefly by Spaniards. Few Cubans were in business on a large scale, as they were content to govern, or practice their professions, if the alien would do the material developing.

It thus befell that with the suppression of Spanish rule Americans saw many opportunities for development. Big steamship companies like the Ward Line, the Peninsular & Occidental, and others; the English-owned United Railways of Havana and the American-owned Cuba R.R. Co.; the National City Bank of New York; the Bank of Nova Scotia; the Royal Bank of Canada; the private Banking House of Gelats & Co.; and other great organizations set about the industrial rehabilitation of the country — which practically had been wrecked by the long war. Millions were spent in terminal facilities (docks, railway stations, etc.), in vast sugar-plantations on which to grow cane, in mills to grind it, and in cars and ships to haul the finished product to market...

Perhaps the greatest American figure in Cuba's industrial development, and a striking illustration of what Cuba offers to men of genius and energy, is the Hon. Frank Steinhart, in 1900 an obscure sergeant in the American Army of Occupation, today a multi-millionaire captain of industry usually referred to as "the man who owns Cuba." His rise to power and fortune was due solely to his inherent good sense, his ability, his integrity, and his consuming will and desire to work. In 1884 these attributes attracted the attention of General William Sherman, who promoted him from sergeant major in the Tenth U.S. Infantry, to be his chief clerk in Chicago. When Gen. Brooke came from Porto Rico to be the military governor of Cuba, he promptly appointed Steinhart chief clerk to the Military and Civil Administration there. In this important position the erstwhile sergeant practically managed the military administration under Generals Brooke and Wood; doing it so efficiently that Gen. Wood publicly referred to him as "my right hand man."

When it was discovered that Steinhart possessed more accurate knowledge of the Cuban character and affairs, and a greater aptitude for organizing and conducting military matters than any of his compatriots, Secretary Elihu Root ordered him to Washington and made him assistant chief of the Insular Bureau. But Steinhart yearned for Cuba, and in due course he was returned there as Special Agent of the War Department. In this new capacity he promptly became diplomatic adviser to, and a buffer between, the United States and Cuba. Greatly admired and implicitly trusted by both countries, he was appointed (in 1903) to the responsible position (which he held until 1907) of American Consul General. His reports on international affairs soon became celebrated for their accuracy, moderation and good sense. His frank and illuminating explanation to Washington of true conditions in Cuba resulted in the Second Intervention and the restoring of peace and progress to the struggling republic under the loyal *Palma* régime. He was the special representative of the great banking house of Speyer & Co. in arranging for a huge American loan to the new Cuban Government, and during the provisional governorship of the Hon. Charles E. Magoon (in 1909) he was publicly thanked for his uniquely valuable services to the two governments.

It is difficult to name a great Cuban development enterprise which Steinhart's constructive genius, his rare judgment, and his money have not at some time aided. Many of the Havana improvements, the excellently managed Havana Electric Railway Company, the Compania Cubana de Electricidad (of which companies he is both President and General Manager), and other big enterprises are due to him. The beautiful Race Course, the incomparable Casino, and several of the finest of Havana's suburbs have felt his Midas touch and guiding hand...

Customs of the country

Customs of the country *(costumbres del pais)* vary with the locality; some are like those of the U.S.; others are Spanish. An oddly comical custom is practiced in some of the eastern towns on a public feast day known as the *Feria de San Juan* (St. John's Fair, or carnival, usually about June 21st, at the period of the summer solstice). On this presumably holy day no one is held physically accountable for whatever hard or bitter things one may say. For folks who harbor grudges it is an ideal sort of safety valve. All the stored-up venom of a year is then mutually released, and vituperative epithets of the most pungent and scarifying nature are freely and enthusiastically exchanged between male and female enemies. Certain of the citizens hear surprising and mortifying things about themselves, their relatives and their ancestors, and each amazed recipient searches his or her soul for a suitable (or unsuitable) retort! All to the uncontrolled amusement of the spectators. At the end of this perfect day, *Fulano* breathes a sigh of relief at having been able to tell *Mengano* and *Zutano* what he thinks of them, as well as the obnoxious woman in the adjoining yard, and he then and there starts accumulating a wider, more expressive, and more scalding vocabulary for the next feast day!

The Carnival

The Carnival (*carnaval*, from *carne*, flesh, and *vale*, farewell), a brilliant season (beginning three days before Lent and dating from the second century, when Bishop Telesphorus, of Rome, instituted a 40-day fast as a rule of the church), is observed in Cuba with marked sumptuousness and amid great rejoicing. The season (which begins the Sunday before Ash Wednesday and continues for the four Sundays following) usually is inaugurated by a magnificent masked ball held in the *Teatro Nacional* and attended by the president of the republic and his suite, and about 5000 representatives of the wealth, beauty and intelligence of Cuba. Visitors can secure admission tickets from influential friends. During the season there are many balls, operas, concerts and other festivals (*verbenas*) in anticipation of the Lenten fasts. On a specified day there is a gorgeous pageant composed of gaily decorated floats which compete for valuable prizes, a crowned queen chosen for her beauty, and a host of masked men and women who pay homage to King Carnival, personified by the mocking *Momus*, and *Terpsichore*, patroness of the choral dance. The scene is one of southern gladness and color difficult to describe. At this time the Paseo de Marti is occupied by a surging multitude of happy people who move in a cloud of confetti, countless miles of tangled paper streamers, and a joyous abandonment...

Havana night life

There is no lack of this in Havana, for the city is not straight-laced. There is no true Bohemian Quarter, but there are allurements, decorous and otherwise, spiritual and sensory. To many the port after midnight is a dusky place devoid of thrills. Those in the know easily find delirious haunts where star-eyed, radiant-faced senoritas and surprisingly emancipated demoiselles dance the winsome and beguiling *habanera* without fear of being pinched by some horse-faced minion of the law... For in this Arcadian Isle, under the free canopy of a sun-splashed or a star-flecked sky, people live their "golden day in an age of iron" less hampered by onerous custom than in certain countries where a drab and circumspect existence is the order of the day. If the northerner finds the Havana night life a bit too saucy, or too strongly reflecting the passionate, insouciant gaiety of sunny southern Spain, it is easily avoided. It also is easy to remember that if the manners and customs of all countries were alike there would be scant reason for, or pleasure in, traveling. As a rule Cubans are generously uncritical about the movements of the stranger within the gates. They work the soft pedal on their own pleasures and rather expect others to do likewise. They are averse to having gloomy, pickle-faced watch-and-warders dog their footsteps about the metropolis, and they prevent their nationals from doing this to the visitor. So that the presence of the ever-alert but friendly policeman expresses a solicitude for one's safety rather than an inquisitorial boring into one's private affairs...

Brothels and harlotry are not supposed to exist in Havana but it is believed that they do. A rather frankly indecorous quarter where the proprieties are violated is that unfragrant region (the oldest section of the port) bounded on the west by the Calle de Economia, on the north by the Calle de la Merced, and on the south and east by the San José wharves. In this confessedly naughty ward are tapestried and mirrored rooms where the salaciously-inclined may witness startling scenes in the flesh or by means of moving pictures. Such places usually are referred to by the cryptic number *soixante-neuf* (Sp., sesenta y nueve, or 69) albeit this number is not that of the houses in question.

The triangular pocket nearest the wharves is a prurient spot resorted to by courtesans varying in complexion from peach white to coal black; 15-year old flappers and ebony antiques; chiefly outlanders who unblushingly loll about heavy-eyed and languorous, in abbreviated and diaphanous costumes; nictitating with incendiary eyes at passing masculinity; studiously displaying their physical charms or luring the stranger by flaming words or maliciously imperious gestures. These gossamer wantons with loving dispositions, who are brutally referred to as *prostitutas,* and more delicately as *celestinas* (celestial bodies!), here practice the scarlet arts... As a rule they appeal only to the hedonist callous to moral degradation or to the lethal consequences of malignantly-poisonous diseases (referred to as *gota militar,* military gout, and whatnot). The bright lights of the Prado shine over a much safer district after nightfall.

Langston Hughes

Cuban Color Lines, 1930

In spite of the fact that Cuba is distinctly a Negroid country, there exists there a sort of triple color line. This triple line, in varying degrees of application, is common to all the West Indies. At the bottom of the color scale are the pure-blooded Negroes, black or dark brown in color. In the middle are the mixed bloods, the light browns, mulattoes, golden yellows and near whites with varying textures of Indian-Spanish hair. Then come the nearer whites, the octoroons, and the pure white of skin. In Cuba, although these three distinct divisions exist, the lines are not so tightly drawn as in some of the other islands of the Caribbean. The British Islands are the worst in this respect. The Latin Islands are more careless concerning racial matters.

But in Cuba one quickly notices that almost all the clerks in the bigger shops are white or near white; that in the daily papers almost all the photographs of society leaders are white, or light enough to pass for white; that almost all the gentlemen who represent the people and sit on government commissions and staff the Cuban consulates and ministries abroad are white, or at least "meriney," as American Negroes term that reddish blond border line between colored and white. But this scale is not 100% true. Occasionally a very dark Negro occupies a very high position in Cuba. That is what misleads many visitors from the United States — particularly colored visitors who are looking anxiously for a country where they can say there is *no color line* — for Cuba's color line is much more flexible than that of the United States, and much more subtle. There are, of course, no Jim Crow cars in Cuba, and at official state gatherings and less official carnivals and celebrations, citizens of all colors meet and mingle. But there are definite social divisions based on color — and the darker a man is, the richer and more celebrated he has to be to crash those divisions.

The use of Havana as a winter playground by American tourists has, of course, brought its quota of Southern racial prejudice from the mainland. Hotels that formerly were lax in their application of the color line now discourage even mulatto Cubans, thus seeking the approval of their American clientele.

But the purely Cuban hotels, with no eye out for tourists, cater to guests of all shades of complexion and the service is most courteous.

My single unpleasant experience in Havana took place at the entrance to the Havana Beach. The Cubans later explained to me that the only wide clean stretch of bathing beach near the city had been leased by politicians to an American concern that built there handsome pavilions and bathing houses for the use of tourists, charged a dollar to go on to the beach — a prohibitive sum then to most Cubans — and proceeded to draw the color line, as well. But since, in Havana, it is very difficult for even North Americans to draw a *strict* color line, the beach often had mulatto politicians and plutocrats sporting thereon. But entrance to the beach then seemed to depend, if you were colored, largely on whether you had enough political pull or social prestige to *force* the management to sell you a season ticket. At the gate, I discovered to my discomfort that they would not sell colored people the customary dollar entrance tickets at all, although they were sold quite freely to whites for a single afternoon's bathing.

If you were colored, the gatekeeper demanded a season ticket.

My friend, José Antonio Fernandez de Castro, and a group of journalists one Saturday had planned a beach party to which Zell Ingram and I were invited. Zell and I, since we had a lot of free time, decided to go to the beach early and spend the whole morning there in the sun until our friends arrived. We got off the street car in front of the tropical entrance pavilion and went to the window to purchase tickets. The young woman at the window said she was sorry there were no tickets. Zell and I stepped back and studied the tariff list posted beside the window. In both English and Spanish the rates for entrance tickets, season tickets, the renting of bathing suits, etc. were clearly printed. Since I speak Spanish I again approached the young lady.

"It says tickets are a dollar each. I'll take two."

She shoved the money back through the wicket. "You'll have to see the manager. I can't sell them to you."

The same sort of treatment had been meted out to me so often in my own country from Kansas to New York, Boston to Birmingham, that I began to understand.

I went to the entrance gate and asked the attendant there to kindly call the manager for me. Instead the attendant called a bouncer. The bouncer was an old American boxer — white, of course — with cauliflower ears and a flat nose.

"What do you guys want? This place ain't run for you," he said. "You can't come in."

"Do you mean to tell me that you're drawing the color line on a *Cuban* beach against *American* citizens — and you're an American yourself?"

"Don't start no arguments," he growled, drawing back his fist.

By now Zell had doubled up his fists, too, and squared off for a fight. Zell was a big fellow, but it seemed better to me not to attempt to settle the matter by a brawl, so I said, "Don't hit him, Ingram." But the ex-pug had already backed up beyond reach.

"Get out," he yelled from within the enclosure, "or I'll send for the police."

"Go ahead," I said, "send for them."

The bouncer retired. A Cuban attendant permitted me to enter the lobby where there was a telephone. I called up José Antonio who asked us to wait there for him; he would be right out by taxi.

As a newspaperman he no doubt scented a story. Zell and I sat down in the lobby to wait. Just then a policeman, at the instigation of the bouncer, came up to us. He was a pleasant young officer, a white Cuban, with apparently little relish for his task.

"*No pueden sentarse aqui*," he said. "You can't sit here."

"Why?" I asked.

"The manager says you can't."

Zell, who spoke no Spanish, kept asking, "Shall I hit him, man?"

"No," I said. "Let's not give them any cause to arrest us. Let José Antonio, who is a Cuban, get at the bottom of this."

"Please get the manager for me then," I requested of the officer.

He went away and shortly returned with the manager, a tall patronizing American white man. I began to explain to the manager why we had come to the beach, but he interrupted to say that we would not be allowed within and insisted that we leave the lobby at once. I said that since it was a public lobby, we would wait there for our friends. The manager declared he would have us ejected.

He went away. Zell and I sat in the big wicker chairs and waited, knowing that it would take perhaps an hour for José Antonio to arrive. Shortly a car sped rapidly up to the entrance, screeched to a halt, and four policemen with drawn sabres jumped out. They came running toward us as if they intended to slice us to mince meat.

"Out!" cried the cops, waving their swords in the air and descending upon us. "Get out!"

In the face of such ferocious weapons there was nothing to do but withdraw, so Zell and I went outside to the platform in front of the pavilion where the street cars stopped. Apparently satisfied the police got back into their car and sped away as we stood by the tracks to wait for our Cuban friends. But shortly the ex-pug appeared again and commanded us to leave the area at once. "Scram! Get going!"

"I'll report this to the American consulate," I said, stubborn and angry by now.

"Report it," cried the pug with a series of oaths. "Go ahead. They won't do nothing."

I knew American consulates had seldom been known to fight the battles of colored citizens abroad if Jim Crow were involved.

"I'll do something," said Zell as his fists doubled up again. This time the bouncer slammed the gate and retreated for good into the beach house. He did not want to fight. Then, in a few moments, with a wail of sirens a large police van swept down the road, stopped in front of us, and a dozen cops leaped out armed to the teeth. This time we were surrounded, hustled into the patrol wagon, and carried off to the nearest station. It happened that the station was in charge of a Negro captain, an enormous, very dark, colored man who listened to the officers' charges against us, wrote them down in his book — and refused to lock us up.

"Wait here for your friends," he said gently. "This is outrageous, but it is what happens to colored people in Cuba where white Americans are in control! This is not the first time there has been trouble at the Havana beach."

Out of breath and quite red in the face after not finding us at the beach, José Antonio arrived shortly, and Zell and I were released from the police station to appear for a hearing on the morrow. To court the next morning the beach authorities sent several Cuban attendants whom we had never seen to present their side of the case to the judge. The attendants swore that Mr. Ingram and I had come into the beach café in our wet bathing suits, had put our feet upon the tables, had used profane language, and had otherwise misbehaved to the discomfort of all the more genteel tourists and bathers.

The judge, a kindly old mulatto gentleman — who might have been termed a Negro had he lived in the United States, but who was "white" in Havana — looked at the beach attendants sternly and said, "These gentlemen, I am sure, never set foot on your beach at all. They had no opportunity to change into their bathing suits. They had not been in the water. The police report indicates that they were arrested fully clothed on the street car platform outside. I believe their statement — that you refused to sell tickets to them — and I do *not* believe your fabrications. What you have done is against all the tenets of Cuban hospitality and against Cuban law, which recognizes no differences because of race or color. These guests on our shores have suffered enough at your hands and deserve an apology. Case dismissed!"

When Zell and I moved on that week to Haiti, our Cuban friends who had invited us to a beach party that never came off gave instead a farewell lobster supper with wine, music, and dancing — so we left Cuba with the rumba throbbing in our ears.

A. Hyatt Verrill

Treasure Island, 1931

To the majority of persons, Guantanamo is known only as the United States naval base, although the town holds many other interests. It was discovered by the Spanish explorers in 1511, yet they took no advantage of it and abandoned the bay, which later became a notorious pirates' nest wherein the buccaneers lay safely at anchor awaiting the Spanish galleons and plate ships passing to and fro between Spain and the Indies.

Why the Dons should have permitted their most feared and dangerous enemies to thus maintain a stronghold in their midst is something of a mystery, but Guantanamo was not unique in this respect, and much of the success of the freebooters was due to the fact that — like parasites — they could maintain themselves almost without interference in the waters ostensibly controlled by those upon whom they preyed.

After the heydey of the buccaneers had passed, the British, under Admiral Vernon, made Guantanamo their base when, in 1741, they were besieging Cuba. Conveniently near Santiago, the bay was a most ideal spot from which to conduct operations against that city. But the stout old Morro prevented the British from taking the town from the sea, and the difficulties of storming it overland were more than the British could overcome...

After the baffled British had sailed away, Guantanamo remained a lonely, almost forgotten spot until 1898, when some 600 American marines landed on the sand dunes at the harbor's mouth and, with little trouble, routed the handful of Spanish soldiers who were supposed to protect the place. From that time on Guantanamo was used as a naval base by the American forces...

Westward from this magnificent harbor, the coast again becomes bold and rocky until, beyond Santiago, it rises in precipitous cliffs culminating in the Sierra Maestra with Turquino's cloud-wreathed summit 8,000 feet above the sea.

It was on this wild, inhospitable, wave-lashed, mountainous stretch of coast that Cervera's ill-fated warships were driven ashore or sunk by the American fleet and, for years after the war, the scarred and battered hulks could be seen scattered along the shores for 45 miles, from Santiago.

At Cape Cruz the shore juts outward in a bold promontory, and tucked away in the corner beyond is Manzanillo, a hot and far from healthful spot, but an important port of a rich, vast agricultural district whose most important inland town is Bayamo... Here Tomas Estrada Palma, Cuba's first president, was born; at the nearby villages of Yara and Baire the lone star flag of Cuba Libre was raised for the first time in the insurrections of 1868 and 1895. In the revolution of 1868 Bayamo was captured by the Cubans, and in the following year, when it was obvious that it must capitulate to the Spanish forces, its inhabitants burned their houses to the ground rather than have them fall into their enemies' hands. In the last insurrection that led to Cuba's freedom there was severe fighting all about the town, and on one occasion the Spanish Captain General — Martinez Campos — narrowly escaped being made a prisoner by Antonio Maceo...

A few miles north of Manzanillo the Cauto River empties into the Gulf of Guacanaybo. Largest and most important of all the island's rivers, the Cauto rises more than 100 miles from its mouth and for half its length is navigable for small steamers. A voyage along this fine stream affords a view of wonderful beauty, with the river banks covered with tropical jungles and dense forests, with tangled lianas and air-plants draping the trees, with orchids gleaming among the foliage and with flocks of egrets, ibis and rose-pink spoon-bills constantly rising from the shallows at the steamer's approach.

Beyond the gulf, with its waters turbid from the river, lie the Gardens of the Queen (*Las Jardines de la Reina*) as Columbus named the scores of islets dotting the turquoise waters... Here the gorgeous flamingoes breed by thousands, their pyramidal mud nests covering the low, swampy shores of many of the *cayos*. Here myriads of ducks, snipe, curlew and other wild fowl flock during the winter. Here the reef-filled sea teems with fish of gorgeous hues and bizarre forms, and here are marine gardens that, seen through the transparent waters, appear like futurists' dreams.

Farther west is Casilda, the port of Trinidad, which is the second oldest town in Cuba having been founded in 1513... Onward toward the west lies Cienfuegos... while still farther westward is Batabano, the port where the traveler boards the steamer for the Isle of Pines... a charming sail of 50 miles...

Discovered by Columbus, the island was named Evangelista, but only on the oldest of maps does this name appear, the present name having been bestowed upon it because of the extensive pine forests that cover a large part of its surface. The Spaniards, who sought gold, a means of getting rich quickly, and an abundance of Indian slave labor, considered the little island worthless and left it to its birds, its alligators and its few aboriginal inhabitants. But with the advent of the buccaneers on the scene, these gentlemen of fortune saw the manifold advantages presented by the pine-covered island so conveniently near Cuba, and they at once established themselves thereon, and from its sheltered bays harassed the Dons for centuries. Then in later years it became a resort for smugglers and when, still later, the Spanish transformed it to a penal colony, the worst criminals of Cuba were added to the choice selection of the island's inhabitants. But as is so often the case, the rascals, when thrown on their own resources and left to themselves, became law-abiding and industrious, and at the close of the Spanish American War much of the land was purchased by Americans, who assumed that the Isle of Pines was destined to become an American possession. Although disappointed in this, they continued to colonize and cultivate the land...

But the most interesting feature of the place is that, almost beyond all question; it is the original of Stevenson's *Treasure Island,* the haunt of Billy Bones and Long John Silver. One has only to glance at a map of the Isle of Pines and compare it with the fanciful map of the novel, in order to see the striking similarity of the real and the imaginary islands. And the visitor to the Isle of Pines will find no difficulty in finding and recognizing the various topographical features of Treasure Island as described in the story. Possibly Stevenson had at some time or another visited the Isle of Pines, and, realizing what an ideal spot it was for a real pirate island, made use of it when he had need of a Treasure Island in his book. Very likely, too, he had heard the innumerable tales of pirates' treasure buried on the Isle of Pines, tales which probably have far more of a foundation of truth than most of their kind, for the island was, as I have said, a resort of buccaneers and pirates, some of whom — more thrifty than their fellows — may possibly have hidden their ill-gotten gains on the place. It is even claimed that no inconsiderable amount of pirates' loot actually has been recovered by treasure seekers. At all events if the freebooters wished to secrete their treasures they could scarcely have found a more ideal spot than the Isle of Pines.

Much of the island is practically unexplored and only a small portion of it has been cleared and cultivated. Over one fourth of the entire area of half a million acres is dense, impenetrable swamp, the home of millions of wild fowl, of alligators, of manatees, and great scuttling crabs. The other three fourths is about equally divided between high mountains, valleys and plains. For the sportsman, it offers many attractions, for the waters of the coast and streams abound in fish; and quail, pigeons, doves, guinea fowl, wild duck, snipe, plover and other game birds are found in the forests, swamps and jungles. Also there is ample opportunity for hunting the huge alligators for which the island has been famed, or I might better say notorious, from earliest times. Even in the buccaneer days these giant saurians were so numerous and so savage as to earn a place in the records of the piratical mariners. In the journal of one of these there is an account of a boat having been capsized and its occupants having been devoured by the alligators, while another mentions a man who fell overboard and was seized and eaten before a rope could be thrown to him...

Aside from its agricultural possibilities, the island possesses numerous mineral springs much of the water from which is bottled and exported to Cuba, where it is consumed in large quantities. There are also numerous mineral deposits, mainly of graphite, copper, silver and manganese, but it is doubtful if any are capable of profitable development. There are, however, valuable marble quarries in the hills, and in the forests are numerous cabinet and other woods, such as mahogany, cedar, lignum-vitae, and of course pine. As the heaviest forests are in the most inaccessible mountainous districts, they hold but scant prospects of being exploited commercially.

But as a winter and health resort, the Isle of Pines holds tremendous possibilities. Its climate is far superior to that of Cuba; it is not over-crowded or overrun by tourists; living is far cheaper than in Cuba; there are more outdoor recreations possible, and, finally, and by no means least important, nearly half of the entire population of 6,000 or more are Americans. Moreover, the island boasts splendid roads, numerous automobiles and large and excellent hotels, while there is no denying that it is one of the most salubrious and most beautiful of tropical islands.

Arnold Samuelson

Aboard the "Pilar" with Hemingway, Havana, 1934

The Morro Castle was only three miles ahead and we would have arrived in 20 more minutes at the usual cruising speed, but with the small motor barely able to hold the boat against the current of the Gulf Stream, we crawled along slowly for two hours and entered the harbor between the stone wall of Morro Castle and the low Havana waterfront at twilight. A launch filled with soldiers in khaki came out to meet us, and ran alongside, a soldier standing with his rifle at parade dress in the bow asking E. H. questions in Spanish. The guards on the lookout tower of the Morro Castle had seen the *Pilar* approach at a good speed until within three miles of land at sun-down, and then it had stopped and approached slowly, acting as if she might be loaded with contraband ammunition for the revolutionaries, afraid to come in before dark. They had sent the soldiers to search the ship. E. H. told the soldiers he was an American yachtsman and fisherman and had come to Havana to fish marlin, and the soldiers replied it was a good story but they had to search the boat anyhow. They were ready to come on board and search when another launch approached and an excited voice shouted, *"!El Hemingway!"*

"!Qué tal, Carlos!" E. H. greeted his boatman.

The soldiers became polite and apologetic when they heard that name. They knew Hemingway as the American millionaire who the summer before had caught 64 marlin with rod and reel and had given away tons of marlin meat to the natives on the dock. They said they had not recognized him in his new yacht, they were sorry they had made the mistake, they hoped he would catch many marlin again this year, and they went away.

The water in the Havana harbor was calm and restful, and everything was new and interesting. We ran in through the channel, past the fishing smacks along the fortress and the ocean boulevard on the Havana side. The channel widened and E. H. stopped near the pier which the fishing smacks used to unload their fish. Lund threw the big anchor off the bow and when it took a hold in the mud, he hitched the rope to the bitt. The incident with the soldiers was over and now when we lay at anchor and had to stay there all night we had time to think about the big motor having broken down. We did not know how long we would be delayed until it could be fixed, or whether E. H. would have to send to the factory for new parts or whether there were mechanics in Havana who could fix it or what the cost might be, and Lund was blaming himself for having run the motors too fast and E. H. might have been silently agreeing with him, although neither of them mentioned it while they talked of other things.

It would have cost $25 extra to clear after six o'clock. E. H. offered to clear if Lund wanted to go uptown to Havana, but he turned the offer down. They talked in the cabin until bedtime and then we all slept on board.

When the customs officers came on board in the morning, they seemed interested only in the way the boat was built, with sleeping accommodations for six people below and a galley and a john and everything, and they didn't try to find hidden ammunition. They opened a few locker drawers as they passed through the cabins without unpacking anything or finding the rifles concealed behind the bunks. E. H. could have had a ton of dynamite under the cockpit deck without it being discovered. The doctor glanced at us and we took down the yellow quarantine flag.

Carlos, the 56-year-old Cuban, wearing a new white outfit with an officer's cap and the letters PILAR sewed across his chest, was standing by in a rowboat with the name *Bumby* painted on its side. When the yellow flag came down, he climbed on board, shook hands with E. H., his black eyes glistening with emotion, and talked excitedly in Spanish, finding the mop and mopping the deck as he talked. There had never been any deck-mopping in Key West. While I watched him mop the deck, I began to lose the comfortable feeling of being useful. I felt the uneasiness of a guest when he sees work being done and wonders whether he ought to help and feels in the way doing nothing. Carlos was getting the attention E. H. had given me when I was his boatman in Key West and E. H., besides being busy with other matters, seemed more reserved; he was now the captain of his ship, an army officer again, and our relationship was becoming less personal because we were on a long expedition together and he had to have discipline.

E. H. went ashore to send a telegram to Pauline, Carlos went along to help find a mechanic, and Charles Lund was in a hurry to get on the ferry, leaving me alone on board.

"Don't worry, you'll see plenty of Havana," E. H. said. "You're not in the navy and you won't be seeing the world through a porthole."

I didn't mind being alone. There was plenty to look at. There was the immense stone wall of the old fortress, running all the way along the narrow channel to the turret of Morro Castle at the point of the harbor entrance, old and gray-looking in the early morning sunlight. There were the passenger boats and freighters from all over the world occasionally coming in and going out of the harbor, seeming to move very slowly because they were so big and leaving a swell that rocked the *Pilar* violently for several minutes after they had passed, and there were many smaller boats — motor launches filled with Cubans and small, slow-moving rowboats with canvas tops over the stern to shade passengers while the oarsman sat toward the bow, rowing backward in the hot sun. On the Havana side, there were the dark faces and white suits of Cubans riding past the gray apartment buildings in small street cars and open automobiles on the waterfront boulevard. There were other Cubans, whose clothes were not so white, standing on the dock nearby, watching men whirl baited handlines around their fingers without having a bite, then throwing the untouched bait far out again.

An old rowboat came toward me and the Cuban in it, wearing more patches than pieces of his original shirt, pointed at the pineapples, grapefruit, and bananas in the bow.

"No speak Spanish," I said.

"Ho Kay," he answered, waving his hands. "Me speak English. Want this? Want this? Want this?"

"How much pineapples?"

"How many want? One five cent. Two ten cent."

"Two," I said, handing him a dime.

"Want wine?" he asked, holding up a quart bottle.

"How much?"

"Forty cent."

"No, that's all."

"You have American cigarette, no?"

"Yes."

"Trade. Wine, one package American cigarette."

"Against the law."

"Me no speak," he said, shaking his head.

"Sorry."

"Two bottles wine, one package cigarette."

"No can do."

"One other day, more pineapple?"

"Sure, come back again."

When I told E. H. about it, he said, "Don't trust anybody. That fellow might have been a government spy trying to get you in bad. You can never tell who they are."

E. H. had returned with several Cubans, all gesturing freely with their arms and shoulders and speaking excitedly as if they were plotting a new revolution, and E. H., now that he was in Cuba where it was the custom of the country talked as loudly and gestured as much as anybody. It was fun watching them talk, although I couldn't make anything out of it except that the water pump of the big motor was causing all the excitement and the rotund man named Cojo who walked on his heels was the mechanic who had come to find out why it did not work. Cojo took the pump apart and told E. H. the metal was burned out and the brass would have to be replaced. He knew metal workers in Havana who could do it, the motor would be as good as new the next morning and it would cost less than if E. H. were in the United States and had to send to the Chrysler factory for a new pump. That was wonderful news. It made everybody happy again, and from then on Cojo was our best friend and the most welcomed guest on board the ship. He was welcome to come along fishing every day and drink himself drunk on good whiskey every night if he wanted to.

In the evening, E. H. was preparing to meet Pauline on board the ferry. He had hired a young Spaniard named Juan who was recommended by the pilots as a good cook, and he left us with this admonition:

"We'll be staying at the Ambos Mundos, so I'll leave you and Juan to watch the ship tonight. Sleep light and if you hear anything get up and see what it is. You've heard us talk about the *Terribles Reglanos.* They're a gang of professional pirates living in Regla, that town over there, and they make their living stealing off American yachts anchored in the harbor. They come across the harbor in the night and they don't make any noise so you've got to be ready for them when they come. You sleep up forward with the pistol under your pillow. They might climb the anchor rope and try the forward hatch. Juan will sleep in the stern with the club. If they come aboard stern first, he'll yell and wake you up, then he'll start clubbing them over the heads till you can get out with the pistol. You'll be down below, so you'll be able to see them and they won't be able to see you. Don't shoot to kill unless you have to. Try to shoot them in the legs but be careful not to shoot any holes in the ship."

"I see. I'll shoot at their knees first, and if they keep coming, I'll raise."

"Chances are the first shot will scare them away because we're so close to the dock, but be sure you've got a full clip."

"It's loaded."

"The moon will be out so they probably won't come tonight, but it's always best not to take chances. How do you sleep?"

"Like a log."

"You can train yourself to sleep light. Even if you don't hear anything, make a practice of getting up a few times in the night anyway and look around to see that everything is all right."

"Okay."

"Is there anything you need on shore?"

"No."

"Then Juan will row me ashore and I'll see you in the morning. Good night."

"Buenos notches."

"That's it. Pick up all the Spanish you can. Juan will make you a good tutor. He speaks pure Spanish."

Juan, hungry-looking, with high cheekbones, hollow cheeks, and shoes that were cracked open, was 30 years old. He was a fiery talker, proud because he was a Spaniard and talked like one and not like a Cuban. He had come over from Spain when he was 18, and cooked on Cuban fishing smacks several years, staying out weeks at a time with no protection against hurricanes. During his last bad storm, he made up his mind that if he ever got out of it alive he would starve to death on land before he would ever go to sea again. When E. H. hired him, he was almost starved, not having had any work for two years. Now he found himself suddenly prosperous, having a job that paid $20 a month and his board, good wages in Cuba, and that night, as we sat together on the afterdeck, he tried to start a conversation.

"*Yo* Juan," he said, pointing at himself. Then he pointed at me, "*¿Usted?*"

"Arnold."

"*¿Cómo?*"

"Arnold."

"Arnold, Engleesh, *muy bien*," he said, nodding his head. "*Pero en español, Arnold, no. Es Arnoldo!*"

"Juan, Spaneesh, very good," I replied. "But in English, Juan, no. It's applesauce."

"*¿Como?*"

"Applesauce." Juan had never known that his name could be changed so much when translated into good English, and he tried to learn to pronounce the word "applesauce" so he could remember it and tell his friends. He was an enthusiastic teacher and scholar, and traded English for Spanish, pointing at the water, the boats, streetcars, automobiles, the moon and the stars and everything else we could see, each giving the names for them as spoken in his own country, soon forgetting the words of the other language and having to point at them again, repeating the words until we could remember some of them, and when we decided to go to bed, Juan appeared well satisfied with our progress.

"*Pronto* Arnoldo speaka *español,* Juan speaka Engleesh," he said. "Watch out for the *Terribles Reglanos.*"

Juan grinned and flourished the club. Hearing the word *"Terribles,"* he knew what I meant.

The *Terribles* did not come that night. At sunrise, I awoke hearing Carlos, barefooted on the cabin roof, mopping the dew off the painted canvas as I used to do in Key West every morning. I went to sleep again and slept until the sun was high enough to come down on me through the forward hatch and the heat made me feel like getting up. Juan was ashore buying food at the market and Carlos, having raised the American flag and cleaned up the ship, was sitting in the stern oiling the big fishing reels. At eight o'clock, E. H. showed up with Pauline to see how things were going, and Carlos, who had seen Cojo, told him the water pump could not be fixed till noon. E. H. said he and Pauline were going for a walk downtown and I was welcome to come along. Carlos rowed us ashore and we walked the narrow, shaded streets lined with buildings cemented together in a solid front against the sidewalks, which were just wide enough for us to walk in single file, with E. H. in the lead taking long steps, Pauline taking short steps behind him, and me in the rear taking medium steps, walking on air. I was having that exhilaration which only comes in full force during your first trip on foot in a foreign city, when everything you have seen before is forgotten, everything you see and hear then being so strange you feel it is the same thing as living again, as if you had died and come to life in a different world.

Erna Fergusson

Afro-Cuban Religious Beliefs, 1946

Dr. Ortiz writes: "The Negro dance shows us the first steps in the evolution of the dance: sensual, exciting, simulating the pursuit and conquest of the woman, it rises to a lively representational finale when sweating bodies, nerves aroused by violent exercise, drink, semi-nakedness, and contact with the opposite sex, end the dance in unrestrained bacchanal. The dexterity of the woman consists in moving the hips voluptuously and harmoniously while keeping the rest of the body almost immobile except for short steps in time with the drum beat or a light vibration in the arched arms whose hands hold the corners of a handkerchief or raise the skirt in accordance with the erotic excitement of the dance. This partial movement is the principal characteristic of the tango. The play of the hips depends upon abdominal contractions which approximate the *danse du ventre*, and the total effect is erotic stimulation..."

To see dances done ceremonially as they originally were in Africa is very difficult. Cubans, both blacks and whites, fear that the United States will get the impression that their country is all Negro and altogether dominated by black magic. But it is fairly easy to see some of the modern manifestations of the ancient African beliefs. Young Cuban intellectuals, all devoted disciples of Dr. Ortiz, know certain shrines, certain *brujos*.

I was taken one night across the star-spangled bay to Regla, said to be a center of witchcraft. In a quiet street we knocked on a door in a house-high wall. A long wait, and then, away inside, a voice and footsteps. The door was opened by a man of clear brown color, very clean, and of light smooth movement. He led us across a patio damp and springy underfoot, rustling with night sounds, and smelling of unseen flowers. A flashlight revealed how moss covered brick copings and ran up the heavy trunk of a ceiba tree. In its crotch perched a small crude statue of Jesus, and at its foot lay a collection of cock-feathers, which have to do with an African cult much older than the worship of Jesus.

The house was dark inside, but our host soon had it garishly lit with an unshaded electric bulb. It was a clean room furnished only with shrines like Catholic altars set in wall niches or built up on plain wooden tables. Each one held a Catholic saint who was also an African deity. Our host pointed out that each one was dressed in a different color and adorned with flowers and candles to match. Santa Bárbara, with her sword, was in red. The Virgin del Cobre's niche was white. That of San Lázaro, no special color. Each, he explained, was invoked for special needs and worshiped at different seasons. He kept insisting that it was all Catholic, though small crude images appeared alongside the saints, as did cock-feathers and shells. The visit was pleasant, but meaningless. Later I found many explanations in Dr. Ortiz's book.

The Virgin del Cobre, as also several other virgins, seems to enjoy a privileged cult as did Obatalá, the superior Yorubá *orisha*, deity. As the Africans believed in an overall deity who was almost never directly invoked, but was approached through lesser *orishas*, the transition from Yorubá to Catholic beliefs was easy. Ignorant slaves, offered the visible symbols of Catholicism, found many things they were used to. They understood that saints had their specialities, and *cofradias*, societies, of the faithful to attend them. They wore fetiches as Catholics wear scapularies. They, like Catholics, recognized and struggled against ill-disposed spirits. But Dr. Ortiz has found nothing to indicate that Africans dealt with the Devil as Europeans did in witchcraft, riding off on broomsticks to meet him or selling out as Faust did. In African witchcraft the spirit is invoked for both good and bad ends; often the evil done is incidental, as when a pain is transferred from a friend to an enemy.

Santa Bárbara is identified with Shangó, an African god of thunder and lightning, who inhabits a palace with bronze doors and showers the earth with meteors. As Santa Bárbara is also invoked against thunder and lightning, bears a sword, and is often shown in a palace like Shangó's, the identification of African god with Catholic saint was easy. The difference in sex is lightly disposed of by the *brujos;* Shangó is Santa Bárbara *macho,* male. In Africa Shangó was hermaphroditic.

I had a personal experience with Santa Bárbara-Shangó, who is working for me right now. The *bruja,* whom I am not permitted to name or locate, took me into a back room where there were altars to San Lázaro (Babalu Aye), the Merced (Oba-talá), and Santa Bárbara. In front of Santa Bárbara was laid a square of red satin, badly worn, and two candles were stuck to the floor. A glass of water stood in front of one candle. The altar itself, built in steps, was bedecked with white and red flowers, many candles, and the image of the saint robed in red.

The *bruja* squatted on the floor. Crossing herself, kissing her thumb, and muttering prayers, she cast a handful of shells on the red satin square. Among them were several that showed carving and one worn coin, *"antiquísimo, Africano."* Over and over she cast them, asking me questions meanwhile. I proved difficult. I could think of no enemies who wished me ill and no diseases that threatened me. No fears assailed me. But at last she got it. I was planning to leave on Sunday. Dreadful! Again she scooped up and cast the little shells muttering with greater urgency, thrusting out her thick lips, wiping her face with her hands in dire despair.

"Ay! Vieja," she wailed, "not Sunday! For the love of God, not Sunday!" Then, turning from me to the saint, she muttered appeals, crying aloud, "San-ta Bár-bara, San-ta Bár-bara," in a tone to break

your heart. Now she was wringing her hands, trying the shells over and over again, rolling her eyes, going rigid, saying words not Spanish. Every time the shells fell into the pattern of a road blocked by danger. She pointed that out; it was unmistakable.

Then, as I remained obdurate about not trying to change plane reservations as she advised, the *bruja* changed her tactics. Now she was casting her shells feverishly, mumbling strange words, scooping and casting, finding always the pattern of that blocked and dangerous road. She fell then into a cataleptic pose, arms and legs rigid, head thrown back, eyes rolled inward, mouth half open. She seemed to be listening intently. I felt altogether forgotten.

The *bruja* came back finally from her trance and reported that Santa Bárbara said that with the sacrifice of a red cock, the passing of more money, the gift to me of a real amber necklace from Africa, all might yet be well.

The *bruja* then summoned her daughter, requisitioned three dollars from me, and sent the girl off to buy the cock. Then she took off her shoes and really got to work. The altar's base was now revealed as a cupboard from which she took a calabash. Muttering the while, she filled the gourd with water, added a dash of perfume, and floated in it a rose and a lily taken from the altar. She also set out a flat dish and laid in it the amber necklace, the shells and coin, and a black wet rock. The daughter returned to report no red cocks available. This added a complication, but the child was sent forth again and the *bruja* visited the other two altars invoking their aid. From San Lázaro's cupboard she extracted a flat dish filled with sand or ashes and set it there.

By this time the room was so filled with magic vibrations that my sponsor, summoned for consultation, was not allowed to enter until a string of ancient African beads had been wound around his arm as a protection. But the daughter entered freely bringing a cock of mottled plumage.

We were now ready for the great final effort. Grabbing the cock by the legs and wings, the *bruja* flourished him before the saint and applied him to my body. Praying unceasingly, she rubbed my head with the bird, then my back and front, arms and legs to the feet. All the time she was crying "Santa Bár-bara! Santa Bár-bara!" beseeching the saint. Then suddenly she would drop her voice an octave into a tone of harsh command and thunder: "Shangó!" It seemed that one could call on the African deity to end all this nonsense and come across, though the Christian saint required supplication. "Shangó! Shangó!" waving the cock on high before the image.

When she was well worked up, she snatched out his breast feathers in big handfuls and piled them on the amber necklace in the dish and around it. The cock let out a couple of squawks, his last. For as deftly as a barman drawing a cork, the *bruja* was quietly twisting off his head. Like one decanting a bottle, and without losing a drop, she poured the thick warm blood over the beads and shells in the dish. She laid the dead head alongside and quickly transferred the cock's body to that ready dish in front of San Lázaro. This mottled cock was the cock of San Lázaro, not of Santa Bárbara. It had been a complicated rite indeed and justifiable only because my determination to leave on Sunday had demanded the utmost speed.

I returned the amber, suggesting that it remain there to keep me under the protection of the saint and the perhaps more powerful Shangó. The coin I kept. It turned out to be a United States dime minted in 1879. Nice of the Catholic Santa Bárbara and the African Shangó to honor it. Obviously they do; my journey, so portentous in anticipation, was easy and smooth.

Patrick Leigh Fermor
Havana Carnival, 1949

The night train from Camagüey to Havana was hurrying us towards the end of our Caribbean journey.

In the south-eastern corner of the island, far beyond the shimmering cordilleras through which we were travelling, lay the city of Santiago, the first capital of Cuba. What a wonderful town it sounds, with its High Renaissance churches in the Florentine style, its Tuscan altars, and its castles, museums, and palaces. It epitomizes for Spaniards who have not crossed the Atlantic all that is most exotic and beautiful in the islands of their lost empire, and it has proved the theme for a poem by Lorca that is almost a metrical litany of nostalgia. Nothing is omitted: the sound of the Trade Winds in the palm trees, the click of the wooden instruments, the rhythm of the dried seeds, the tobacco flower, the alligators:

Cuando llegue la luna llena iré a Santiago de Cuba
Iré a Santiago
En un coche de agua negra.
Cantaran los techos de palmera
Iré a Santiago...

(When the moon is full, I will go to Santiago de Cuba
I will go to Santiago
In a coach of black water.
The roofs of the palm trees will sing
I will go to Santiago.)

The moon that hung so low over the mountains was as full, as expanded as it is possible for the luminary to be; filled to the point of brimming over, as it were, with lunar substance, until only a circumference 10 times her normal size could accommodate it; a lamp that drowned the lustre of every star and quickened the wild surrounding mountain ranges and every tree of the unflurried woods that throve in the valleys; and, with the same impartiality struck everything dead. The branches hung with a metallic and thunderstruck rigidity, and only the sleek elongated reflections of the moon in the railway lines were subject to movement or change.

A strange landscape rose from the mists of the dawn. It was a vista of symmetrical and juxtaposed hemispheres of pale green, and each mound was placed in relationship to its neighbours with the precision of a cell in a honeycomb. The white mist still lingered in the ravines, so that the country rolled away in an infinity of green discs floating on a pale and softly moving network. Across this vague landscape the Royal Palms wandered away in Indian file, each of them taller and more slender than any imaginable tree. This wonderful plant, the *Orodoxia Regia*, is indigenous to Cuba, and it has become the emblem of the Republic. It appears again and again in the embossed and gilded panoramas inside the lids of cigar-boxes; those landscapes that so faithfully capture, as truth is captured by a parable, the atmosphere of Cuba. The smooth trunk, grey-green and perfectly cylindrical, shoots into the air to a phenomenal height, and, on its journey, swells and diminishes with the most gentle curves like the pillar of an Egyptian temple with its girth melted to the exiguity of a pencil and its length drawn ever higher into the sky to explode there in a miraculous corolla of leaves. These dark masses of foliage hung like enormous birds flying parallel to the track of the train or migrated in long winding flights towards the primrose and scarlet daybreak. Isolated *haciendas* floated past with the columns of their verandahs lost in the mist, surrounded now and then by palm-thatched colonies of huts. The little stations were thronging with Negroes and Mulattoes waiting for a later train to Havana: white assemblies of sombreros that all slanted upwards and rotated together as the express rushed past and above them. Yards full of ox-carts appeared for a few seconds, and heavily-caparisoned horses up to their hocks in mist. Then the tobacco-fields or a sudden lake of sugarcane swept them away, and the strange ballooning savannah returned once more. Grey cattle meditated on the convexities under the palms or moved along the misty labyrinth like ghosts of which only the great emerging horns were real.

The humble *Perla de Cuba* had infinitely more charm than the luxury palaces that abounded in the more fashionable quarters of Havana. My great wooden bed was more elaborate and unwieldy than a Spanish galleon, and there was something pleasingly austere and monkish about the bare white stone walls of the room and the high ceilings. A single metal spigot fed the washbasin with water. The basin itself was a shallow fluted scallopshell of marble, destined, one would have said, more for some symbolic sacerdotal purpose than for any mundane ablutions. During the heat of the afternoons, this tall white cell was a priceless refuge. Safely immured here behind closed shutters from the glare and the dust, I would lie and read the history of the Spanish empire. A jug of ice-cold beer stood within easy reach and only a muted suggestion of the traffic penetrated the cool and watery dimness. A ship's siren was audible now and then and every quarter of an hour the bells of Havana sounded. The sweetness of their tone, the Cubans say, is due to the quantities of silver and gold that their ancestors poured into the molten bronze when the bells were cast three centuries ago.

What an astonishing race of men these early Spaniards were! As I turned the pages of the chronicles and histories that record their gestures, the shadowy bearded figures assumed reality and life...

Volume after volume is filled with the expeditions through the jungles in full plate armour, the battles with the Indian hosts, the victories and disasters, the sudden astounding visions of Popoca-tepetl and Chimborazo. The mind winged forward to these new realms, to the caciques and emperors in their palanquins of parrots' feathers, the warriors armed with weapons of chalcedony and obsidian, the cathedrals and the grandees' palaces which sprang up in the jungle. Their adventures made it hard to restrict one's thoughts to the confines of this island from which so many of them had set forth; from which, in a couple of days, we were to follow them.

The end of carnival coincided with our last night in Cuba. We forced a passage through the mob which thronged the sides of the Prado, the great boulevard that runs into the central square under the dome of the Capitol, and sat on the kerb with a family of Cubans. Decorated grandstands receded behind us in tiers, and the small boy beside me pointed out the President and other prominent figures. Posses of police roared up and down the empty street on motorcycles, it all seemed too organized and civic for a carnival. The first beauty-queens, floating at a snail's pace on edifices like huge wedding-cakes of tinsel through dutiful outbursts of clapping, augured badly. It looked as if the whole thing might turn out to be a bore. Hold-ups of three-quarters of an hour turned the effulgence of their smiles to cardboard, and the bare arms that waved in acknowledgement of the languishing plaudits lent to the triumphal cars the purposeless, fluttering motion of sea anemones. They shrank, as the clapping subsided, into immobility, to unfurl and wave again only when the cortege moved on.

At last the final chariotload of Venuses sailed by, and a fanfare of trumpets heralded the arrival of a far stranger procession organ-ized by the Chinese community of Havana. Little men in the cos-tumes of Buddhist priests swelled their cheeks over the mouthpieces of long wind instruments resting on the shoulders of the boys in front of them. A cohort of pikemen followed. They were dressed from head to foot in Chinese armour and they grasped in their hands long halberds with fantastically shaped blades. After them came standard-bearers with silk banners which were embroidered and tasselled and fringed and charged with gleaming stars and with dragons. Others bore aloft on poles enormous three-dimensional dragons made of paper, lit from inside and spiked along their backs, with beams of light blazing from their eye-sockets; resplendent pterodactyls whose tails uncoiled for many yards overhead.

Other light-bearers accompanied them, supporting, in the slots of their baldricks, poles 10 or 15 yards high that poised on their summits many-coloured parchment globes. Some of them were several yards in circumference, the upper parts tapering into the air like pagodas. The curling gables of the superstructure were strung with coloured lights and tassels and bells and Chinese ideograms were painted on their illuminated parchment panels. As they moved along, the light-bearers twirled the staves in their sockets, and the airy palaces and temples, glowing with a soft lustre against the stars, swung and gyrated high over our heads to the sound of bells and trumpets and far-oriental music.

There was something unspeakably charming and almost magical about this flimsy flying architecture. Chinese girls in gold litters came after them, and then, trotting among pikemen, little piebald horses splendidly caparisoned, and miraculously emerging, one would say, from the T'ang dynasty. They bore upon their backs fairy-tale Manchu princesses whose heavy silk and gold-embroidered robes, sweeping to the ground with the stiffness of metal, entirely enveloped them. Under winged and pinnacled headdresses, ivory Chinese faces of extreme beauty gazed into the night, as motionless and grave under their gleaming accoutrements as those saints on ikons of the Eastern Church whose faces and hands alone the silverwork reveals.

Like a length of Chinese embroidery the procession coiled away. The sound of the bugles and bells grew fainter, and the shining edifices receded; a diminishing Chinese Venice floating into the distance on a lagoon of stars.

An African sound now struck our ears: the clatter and boom of tom-toms, the sneezing jerk of the shack-shack and the scraping of plectrums over slotted gourds; and, again in the wake of a forest of lights and escorted by the flames of torches, an interminable but orderly horde of Negroes came dancing down the street. They heaved backwards and forwards with the advance and the recoil of the authentic Negro dance of Cuba: the *Conga*. On they came in hundreds, each dancer evolving alone; surging three paces to the left, stopping with a sort of abrupt choreographic hiccup on a half beat, then three paces to the right (crash!), and then to the left again as all the barbaric instruments underlined the beat. As the impact of the music grew, the approaching dancers themselves increased every second in size, until they were dancing past like an invasion of giants.

They were tall, jet black Negroes and handsome Negro women in the slave costume of the plantations. The latter were dressed in white blouses and red billowing skirts with three rows of frills. Red scarves were tied round their heads and tartan shawls about their shoulders. The men were barefoot and sashed with scarlet. Their trousers ended in a fringe half-way down their calves, and a length of tartan stuff was bound about their loins. At their waists hung a tin cup and a plate and red handkerchiefs were tied round their foreheads under broad-rimmed wicker hats of which the front of the brim was fastened back with a large black scorpion. Enormous scorpions were also painted on the drums and banners, and below them were hung scarecrow figures of 18th century plantation owners in powdered wigs. Each of the dancers held in one hand a length of green sugarcane and in the other a cutlass which he flourished in rhythm with his steps. They were singing a deep repetitive African chant that rose and fell and abruptly ceased and then began all over again in the mode of a Voodoo incantation or one of the Koromantee songs of the Maroons.

In the middle of the throng danced the drummers, some with toms-toms slung from their shoulders and others moving along locust-fashion with their instruments between their bent knees. Troops of Negroes carried drums on their shoulders that were seven yards long; cylinders, like the Assotor drums of the Haitian forests, hollowed from the boles of large trees. Held high above the heads of the dancers, the drummers crouched forward astride these great instruments like demoniac jockeys, the palms of their hands beating the drumheads of membrane with a frenzy that sent each blow booming down the cavern of the drum and out into the air like a shot from a cannon. In this stupendous *Conga,* there was nothing frivolous or carnivalesque. The combination of dance and symbol and song was in the nature of a summing-up of the history and the revolts of the Negroes and of the lament for Africa. It was an apocalyptic intimation, too, of Voodoo, Obeah, Cambois, Schango, Nanigo, Los Santos, Batonga-Naroca, Candomble, Caboclo, Ubanda, Macumba, and Wanga and all the secret Negro cults of the Americas, and the admiration evoked by the precision and the abandon of the dancing and the magnificent volume of the singing and of the music of the drums was closely allied to awe.

Gradually the Scorpion dancers moved on. They were succeeded, as the hours passed, by armies, each of them over a hundred strong, of Negroes and Mulattoes. First came a party of mock Spaniards in Andalusian dress. Then a Harlem group. The men sported top-hats and tail-coats and gold-knobbed canes and danced gravely along with cigars between the white gloved fingers of their right hands. On the sleeve of their gallantly crooked left elbows rested the gloved arms of their partners: tubes of silver or scarlet or lilac attached to sinuous figures in superbly exaggerated evening dresses that might have been designed by Balenciaga. From the naked shoulder to the knee, they clung as tightly as snakeskin and then flared out behind the stilt-heeled golden shoes in peacock's tails of coloured feathers and sequins. Panaches of ostrich-plumes rose from hip and shoulder and the towering Carmen Miranda head-dresses, ascending from their sleek coiffures and climbing and branching and expanding in the air like multi-coloured pineapple foliage, tossed and coruscated with each advancing step.

Then came the Dark Town Strutters; the blazered and straw-hatted, banjo-strumming minstrels; *Charros* and *Vaqueros* with big spurs and sombreros; conquistadores in full armour, musketeers, courtiers in silk and brocade, animals, tumbling dwarfs, and a hunch-back with his head flung back who, for mile after mile, balanced a glass of water on his forehead. As the last troop passed the Capitol, the spectators surged round and among them, and the procession simultaneously fanned out and disintegrated among the crowd in many brilliant islets of colour; all, dancers and crowd alike, swelling and seething and shuffling in a dazzling confusion, until the town became a universal *Conga* under a heaving roof of lanterns and streamers and confetti, and stars.

Holding hands lest the human currents should carry us off into different maelstroms, we headed back to the *Perla de Cuba* to collect our luggage. Breaking free from the main tide of dancers, we raced along the back streets, for our plane was leaving in half an hour. The rum-shops in the colonnaded lanes were packed to capacity with disguised Negroes. A party of Scorpions, with their cutlasses scattered about the tables, were drinking straight out of the bottle. One of their number still hammered away at a drum while a Mino-taur span round and round, slowly clapping his hands. Confetti was scattered everywhere and tangled balls of streamers had collected in the gutters. Under a street lamp at the corner six amazing figures stood in colloquy. They were horses' heads 10 feet high, like gigantic chessmen with bared teeth and staring eyes, their lower lips, articulated to mimic the action of speech, hanging inanely loose. Little portholes in their breasts revealed the faces of six Negroes smoking cigars. Intrigued by our three running figures, the great heads swung ponderously round and followed us out of sight with their great fatuous eyes.

The lights of Havana grew smaller and finally merged into a luminous smear. The only distinguishable object was the revolving beam of the lighthouse on the Morro, and in a little while we were flying over a bare tract of the Caribbean. The aeroplane was almost empty. Joan and Costa, exhausted like me by the doings of the last few hours, had turned off the lights over their seats and settled down to sleep. I felt I should soon do the same. The water was scarcely visible by the light of the stars, but in a little while the remains of a moon began to appear and a faint radiance was spread over the eastern rim of the sea...

Frank Ragano and Selwyn Raab

In Havana with The Mafia, 1958

On my first trip alone, Santo met me at the airport with a Cuban friend and casino partner, Evaristo Garcia. Santo and Garcia were the principal owners of the Commodoro Hotel and casino, one of the places into which the Trafficante family had put money in the late 1940s. On the drive into Havana, they talked about the best place for me to stay.

Garcia turned to Santo and said, "Why don't we put Frank up in the special suite at the Commodoro?"

The two of them burst into laughter.

"It's obviously a private joke," I said. "What's the special suite?"

Santo, the expression on his face now serious, remarked that in the previous year, 1957, he had met Senator John F. Kennedy of Massachusetts while the senator was visiting Havana. His instinct told him Kennedy had a yen for the ladies and he and Garcia offered to arrange a private sex party for him, a favor Santo thought might put the prominent Kennedy in his debt.

They set up the senator with three gorgeous prostitutes in the "special suite" at the Commodoro. It was special because a two-way mirror allowed Santo and Garcia to secretly watch the proceedings from an adjoining room.

Recounting the story Garcia's face crinkled in smiles while Santo remained deadpan. Observing a respected U.S. senator cavorting in bed with three call girls was one of the funniest sights they had ever witnessed. Because Kennedy had accepted their offer, Santo and Garcia had lost all respect for him. From their point of view, an official like Kennedy, who publicly preached law, order, and decency and secretly took bribes or slept with prostitutes was a rank hypocrite who deserved no esteem.

Santo was no Peeping Tom, and from the way Garcia laughed, I considered him to be the chief culprit in arranging the orgy.

Santo enjoyed a royal lifestyle in Havana. His wife, Josephine, whom he always referred to as Josie, and their two daughters, both of whom were schoolteachers, lived in Tampa and rarely visited him. He luxuriated in a vast apartment he owned in a chic 25-story building with a panoramic view of Havana and the Malecón, the broad boulevard along the city's scenic harborfront.

For female companionship Santo, who was in his mid-forties, kept a Cuban mistress, Rita, a former showgirl at one of his nightclubs, who was some 20 years his junior.

"I've got a wonderful wife," he said matter-of-factly, "but everybody in Cuba has a mistress, even Batista. You've got to have fun in this world."

Santo and his father had been operating casinos in Havana since 1946, and their investments multiplied enormously after Fulgencio Batista seized power in a 1952 coup d'état. Everyone knew that Batista's government was thoroughly corrupt. Although he exacted a heavy price from the casino and hotel operators, Batista rewarded them richly. Tourism and gambling were priorities for Batista and he encouraged their growth. Visa requirements were waived to make it easy for Americans to spend time in Cuba, and with the expansion of the airline industry, Havana became a favorite playground for

Americans. Batista unintentionally led the boom in tourism and gambling that later transformed the Caribbean.

More tourists meant more action in the casinos, and to help the Havana casinos compete with Las Vegas, the government permitted 24-hour gambling and no limits on wagers. Government controls and supervision of the gaming rooms were minimal. Of course, all casino operators had to kick back sizable sums in return for the unrestricted privilege of providing blackjack, dice, roulette, and slot machines to players.

The cost of a government gambling license was nominally $25,000 but Santo explained that $250,000 was the expected amount to be paid under the table for a lucrative concession.

Each casino was visited almost nightly by bagmen who collected a percentage of the take for Batista and his cronies.

One of the first casino entrepreneurs in Cuba, Santo by 1958 had established the largest gambling network in Havana. It was all legal. He either owned or was the head of syndicates that controlled five casinos. One was in a nightclub, the Sans Souci, and the remainder in the Capri, Commodoro, Deauville, and Sevilla Biltmore hotels. (The mob had a penchant for continental names.)

Except for the Commodoro, all were relatively new and had opened in the last decade.

At the Capri, George Raft, the movie tough guy of the thirties and forties, worked as a "greeter" who glad-handed and joked with the customers. Santo said Raft's charm and his reputation as a movie star were good for business, drawing customers who came to see him and stayed to gamble.

It was Santo's heavy investments in these five places, he said, that left him short of cash and compelled him to seek Anastasia as a partner in his unsuccessful bid to raise $2 million for the Havana Hilton casino concession. The Hilton lease was eventually given to a group led by a Cuban millionaire and business partner of Batista.

I never gambled and neither did Santo, although sometimes when asked for his occupation he described himself as a gambler.

"Bartenders don't drink because they see the consequences," he told me. "I know how the odds are stacked against the players. You can't beat the casinos."

On my first night in Havana, Santo took me on the rounds of several of his casinos. His favorite was the Sans Souci because it had a nightclub and floor show that was one of the most popular draws for Cubans and tourists.

We visited the nightclub shortly before the first show was to start and Santo gave me a backstage tour. He strolled into the chorus girls' dressing room where many of the dancers and singers were half nude and barebreasted. While I was uncertain about what to do with my eyes, Santo casually chatted with the girls in Spanish, which he spoke fluently. When he introduced me to some of his favorite performers, none exhibited any embarrassment.

In the men's dressing room, all the dancers and singers in a state of undress immediately covered their genitals.

Outside, I asked Santo, "Why are these guys running for cover? The girls didn't."

"You don't know? They're queers," he said, grinning at my naiveté. The men, who never performed in the nude, did not want to expose themselves to heterosexual men.

The next stop was the casino's counting room. A uniformed guard stood outside as Santo pulled out a key and unlocked the door to a small room, about 12 feet square, containing a wide table and a huge safe. The casino was air-conditioned but the room was stuffy, a floor fan providing only a warm breeze.

Two men, one wearing a green head visor and the other making entries in a ledger, were at a table covered with stacks of U.S. money.

"This is Henry," Santo said, introducing me to the man working on the ledger with an adding machine. "This is the most important room in any casino. We deal in cash and either you make it or lose it by what goes on in this room. Henry here is from Tampa and he watches that the count is right and that nothing gets lost. These people will steal you blind," he added, referring to the Cuban employees. "So I bring people from Tampa to watch the counting room."

On that first trip, I also accompanied Santo as he made his late rounds of the casinos. One night, close to dawn, he pointed out a visitor as the bagman for Batista's wife. She got 10 percent of the profits from the slot machines in all of Santo's places. "You pay for everything in Havana," he said without rancor.

Impressed by his holdings in Havana, I asked him why, since he was so successful legitimately in Cuba, he did not turn an honest dollar at home.

"Frank, a man who is blind in one eye has a great deal of vision among the blind," he said with a wide smile. In other words, corruption and loose standards made it easy for him to prosper in Cuba.

The other major gambling impresario in Havana was Meyer Lansky, the partner and close friend of Lucky Luciano. Lansky organized the syndicate that built the Riviera Hotel, one of Havana's largest, and the lavish new Gold Leaf Casino at the hotel. With his brother Jake, Lansky controlled another major casino, the Internacional, at the Hotel Nacional de Cuba, and the Montmartre Club, a casino with a reputation for attracting serious high rollers who cared little for gaudy floor shows.

Santo paid all my expenses in Havana and on one trip put me up at the Riviera instead of one of his hotels. I thought he had done so because he was friendly with Lansky, but it turned out that he just wanted me to get a look at one of Havana's poshest places.

At dinner that night I brought up Lansky's name and asked if he lived in the Riviera. Santo turned frosty. "That dirty Jew bastard, if he tries to talk to you, don't have anything to do with him. My father had some experiences with him and you can't trust him."

Santo never mentioned Lansky's name to me again. Back in Tampa, when I inquired discreetly among Santo's lieutenants, they said Santo's father had considered Lansky a dangerous potential rival in Cuba and that Santo despised him. I could only wonder how these two men, the most important overseers of mob investments in Havana, could function without getting along smoothly with each other and having mutual interests.

After several visits I had to agree that Havana was the most fantastic city in the world. It had everything — glamour, a great climate, excellent food, and an incredible nightlife.

An essential ingredient of Havana's ambience was its spectacular nightclub shows. Santo's Sans Souci had both an indoor club for rainy days and an outdoor club where, in good weather, shows were staged for audiences of 500. As in all the clubs the show at the Sans Souci continued without intermission from 8:00 p.m. to 4:00 a.m. Extra musicians were always ready to relieve the performers so that the music never stopped. Platforms were built on the palm trees surrounding the stage and 40 to 50 dancers in elaborate, revealing costumes were illuminated as they performed dazzling routines there.

Sex was a big drawing card for the tourists and some motels in

Havana rented rooms for 15 minutes or a half hour — a practice that would come to America two decades later. The Cubans knew that some couples did not need an entire night to enjoy themselves. To ensure privacy, high walls were built around the motels so cars could park unseen.

Santo got a kick out of showing me around, introducing me to the eroticism that was unavailable in the States. He thought I was a bit innocent, not a man of the world. I became a different man in Cuba. In Havana, my traditional values seemed less important, and Santo's became more honest and less hypocritical than those of most people. He extracted all the pleasure he could out of life without the slightest twinge of moral guilt and he was absolutely uncritical of himself. I wanted to fit into his life, emulate him, gain his respect. Had he made a conspicuous effort to remodel my character I might have resisted him, but his influence was subtle. By remaining true to his own nature, he changed the course of my life.

I am Sicilian enough to acknowledge that, to me, respect is the most significant factor in a relationship between two men. So long as I respected Santo, he was the chief role model in my life.

I sometimes wondered if I had discarded all my ethical standards in Havana. Then I would reflect on Santo's theme that Havana's lifestyle was created to be enjoyed, and since everyone else was savoring its delights, why should I be the exception?

Havana was famous for *los exhibiciones* — sex shows — and Santo thought I should see one, assuring me that I would see the most select one available, offered only to the privileged cognoscenti.

"We don't want to go to the tourist traps," he said. "The first thing every secretary, schoolteacher, and nurse wants to see when they come here is *la exhibicion.*"

Santo drove to a house in one of Havana's better neighborhoods and the woman who opened the door was obviously expecting him. A Cuban who spoke good English, she wore a low-cut evening gown. She escorted us to a room that had been converted into a cocktail lounge with a bar and tables. "When you gentlemen are ready to see a show, let me know," she said.

While we waited for drinks, Santo gave me another lesson on Havana's demimonde. Normally, he said, the shows were presented to groups of six to eight people, either a single party or couples who had arrived separately.

"There is a room across the hall where they present three men and three women and you select a pair who will be the performers. The charge is $25 per person — pretty cheap considering what kind of show they put on."

Santo had arranged a private performance for the two of us, and after our second drinks arrived, we said we were ready and carried the drinks with us into another room. The hostess silently introduced three men and three women wearing thin robes. In unison, they opened their garments, presenting their bodies for our inspection.

"We want El Toro and that girl over there," Santo told the hostess, pointing to a curvaceous woman with well-rounded and firm breasts.

Nodding, the hostess asked us to follow her into an adjoining room furnished with couches and settees for about a dozen people. A crescent-shaped platform surrounded by wall mirrors served as a stage. The other walls were hung with paintings of nude men and nude women, all of them amply endowed.

The hostess clapped her hands and El Toro and the woman entered in the nude and began the performance on quilts spread out on the platform, which was lighted like a real stage. They engaged each other for 30 minutes in every conceivable and contorted position possible and concluded with oral sex.

I was shocked to the core but tried to appear blasé to impress Santo. When it was over, Santo and I went back to the cocktail room for another round of drinks.

"What did you think of that show?" he asked.

"It was incredible. How can people do that for a living?"

"Frank, you've got to remember, over here there's something for everybody. You want opera, they have opera. You want baseball, they have baseball. You want ballroom dancing, they have ballroom dancing. And if you want sex shows, they have live sex shows. That's what makes this place so great."

El Toro was a man in his mid-thirties, about six feet tall and average-looking except for his genitalia. "Yeah," Santo said. "His cock is supposed to be about 14 inches long. He's quite a guy. They also call him 'Superman.'"

Home movies was a hobby of mine and I thought Superman's performance would make a terrific erotic film. Santo obtained permission for me to privately film the great man in action; I still have the footage, probably the only movie made of Superman. After witnessing the second performance, I chatted with Superman, who had a fairly good command of English. He told me he earned about $25 a night.

"You come to Miami," I said jestingly. "I'll get you a pair of those loose, short shorts. We'll walk up and down the beach in front of the hotels. I guarantee you that you'll end up owning one of the big hotels." Superman laughed but he stayed in Havana where, according to a popular joke, he was better known than President Batista. Two decades later, he was immortalized in America's popular culture, although it failed to enrich him. In a scene in the film *Godfather II*, the mobsters are in Cuba, watching a sex exhibition, and there is a reference to a phenomenon known as "Superman." That scene was more accurate than the audience realized.

Every time I came to Havana I was given another lesson in the city's supply of sexual diversions. Martine Fox, the owner of the Tropicana nightclub, who produced the most popular shows in Havana, was Santo's friend. Through Santo's influence I was seated at a choice table with Martine one night at the Tropicana. The show's theme was "Miss Universe," and Martine offered me any girl in the show. "Take your pick," he said. "You want two girls? Three girls? Anything you want." Logically, the most beautiful woman in that show had to be the "entry" from Cuba, so I told Martine I wanted "Miss Cuba," sight unseen. After the show he escorted a stunningly beautiful woman to my table. She was Miss Cuba, my date for the remainder of the evening.

Martine then suggested that we see an unusual show that he set up for me at the Commodoro. The entertainers were all women, and they performed lesbian acts and offered to make love to men in the audience. Martine told me that many men found watching lesbian sex more stimulating than the heterosexual shows.

I was working hard in Tampa, with cases going all the time, and no pause for relaxation. My compensation was Cuba. I had an open invitation to be Santo's guest there whenever the mood struck me.

Although rumors abounded in Cuba that Santo was a drug kingpin, I never saw him use or sell drugs. He told me that the Cubans thought he was involved with drugs because his family name meant "trafficker" in Spanish. He made a joke out of it, dismissing the Cubans as gullible.

One of Santo's socialite friends, Alfredo, came from a prominent

Cuban family and Santo took me to several of his lavish parties for Havana's social elite.

Alfredo had dozens of mistresses, each one living in a large villa he provided. A joke circulating in Havana was about Alfredo and his collection of love nests. Someone would ask what business he was in. The reply was, "Oh, he's in real estate."

Most of the voluptuous and statuesque beauties in the nightclub productions were only 14 or 15 years old. Alfredo and I were in a supper club watching the floor show one evening when a middle-aged woman approached him, introduced herself, and pointed out a young girl in the audience. "That's my daughter. Can you take care of her? She'll be glad to be your mistress." Alfredo refused; he told her he had all the mistresses he needed. "Please," the woman pleaded, "can't you just meet her?" She was again rebuffed. I was amazed that a mother would so brazenly offer him her daughter, but Alfredo shrugged; this was a common occurrence for him.

I watched my drinking carefully when I was around Santo, recalling his distaste for Pat Whitaker's escapades with alcohol. I knew he was measuring what he considered my "control" in Havana and I almost failed the test.

One night Santo, tied up with business, suggested I spend the evening with Alfredo at the Sans Souci. Trying to show my manliness, I kept pace with Alfredo's enormous capacity for drink. Although he was in his fifties, at least 10 years older than I, I was no match for him. He frequently went to the men's room, returned, danced the cha-cha, and ordered a fresh round.

I was on the verge of passing out when Santo appeared. "You're drunk," he said.

I told him I had tried to keep up with Alfredo and failed. Laughing, Santo said, "Come with me, I want to show you something." He led me to the men s rest room and unlocked a door at the back of the room to reveal a wall filled with safety deposit boxes. Inside the boxes the rich Cubans kept their private stashes of cocaine, effective as pep pills when they were nightclubbing. Alfredo had dosed himself whenever he visited the men's room.

"That guy will be partying for the next two or three days," Santo said. "Don't bother trying to keep up with him."

Later I had second thoughts about the implications of those boxes filled with cocaine in Santo's club. They lent fuel to the rumors that dogged him at home and in Cuba that he and his family were drug dealers, but I never saw any other evidence that Santo was involved in narcotics.

Despite the seductive excitement and decadence surrounding him, Santo seemed to be placid and untroubled in Havana. He drank moderately and kept himself in reasonably good shape. Life was delicious for him in Havana and he was the living fulfillment of an adolescent boy's dreams.

Santo had lawyers in Cuba and Pat Whittaker still represented him as chief counsel in Florida, but he established a pattern of asking my opinion on legal and business matters in Cuba and in Florida. And he continued to refer clients to me at home.

One afternoon late in 1958 I was at the Columbia restaurant in Tampa and overheard Santo's brother Sam talking about Santo. "I hope to hell my brother knows what he is doing," Sam said. "All the money we're making is going down there, to Cuba."

In Cuba, Santo informed me about hotel business deals he was working on and several times suggested I invest in them. A new casino was being planned by his friends in 1958, with shares being sold privately at $25,000 for each one percent or point of the total investment.

"Buy a few points, you'll get rich," Santo advised, adding that Cuba was a better place than the United States to invest money for fast and large profits.

I discussed the proposals with my wife, Betty, but she said, "Hasn't Santo heard about that revolutionary, Castro? He's trying to take over Cuba."

When I mentioned Fidel Castro and his insurrection to Santo, he sneered. Castro, he assured me, was a joke, but just in case the unexpected happened, he and his friends were secretly contributing to the rebels as well as to Batista. Santo figured that no matter who won the war, he would emerge safe and sound. All his bets were covered.

"I'm sure Fidel Castro will never amount to anything," Santo said. "But even if he does, they'll never close the casinos. There is so much damned money here for everybody."

Late in December 1958, Santo telephoned me at my office from Havana, inviting my wife and me to come down as his guests for the New Year's Eve celebration. American newspapers were full of accounts of Castro's military victories and of bombings in Havana.

"Santo, I don't think it's a good idea to go now," I replied. "The newspapers say Castro is about to take over."

"Nonsense! He's got the mountains. He's a guy making noises up in the hills. He's going nowhere. Don't worry about him. We'll have a good time."

notes on the authors

Exquemelin

Alexander O. Exquemelin was born in about 1645. His nationality is uncertain, but he was likely a native of Harfleur in France. He settled in Holland after serving three years with the French West India Company in Tortuga after 1666, then with the buccaneers, perhaps as a barber-surgeon, until 1674. His book, originally in Dutch as *De Americaensche Zee-Roovers*, appeared in 1678, and its author died after 1707. This extract, translated from the original by Alexis Brown, is taken from *The Buccaneers of America*.

Ballou

Maturin M. Ballou (1820-95) was one of the founders of the *Boston Globe*. He first visited the island in 1854, and his *History of Cuba* presents a wealth of detail about Cuban daily life, while his version of the Marti episode shows he certainly had a newspaperman's eye for a good story. A later book titled *Due South or Cuba: Past and Present* appeared in 1885, reprising accounts of Ballou's earlier travels, including his dramatic first-hand encounter with a slave ship.

Hawthorne

Sophia Peabody Hawthorne (1809-71) sailed to Cuba around late 1833, early 1834, hoping the island's mild climate would improve her health. Happily, this proved to be the case, and she married the novelist Nathaniel Hawthorne soon after her return home. This letter was preserved in her *Cuba Journal, 1833-35*.

Bryant

A former lawyer turned poet and journalist, William Cullen Bryant (1794-1878) eventually became editor of the *New York Evening Post*, where his letters home from Cuba were first published before they were collected in *Letters of a Traveler, or Notes of Things Seen in Europe and America* (New York, 1850).

Dana

Richard Henry Dana Jr (1815-92) was the author of *Two Years Before the Mast,* and following his first book's success, became a lawyer specializing in maritime cases. His visit to Cuba in 1859 was brief, and his impressions dashed off at speed, but *To Cuba and Back* became another best-seller, and is distinguished by its liveliness and freshness of observation.

Dimock

Little is known about Joseph J. Dimock. He was born in Virginia in 1827 and was a commercial agent in Boston before marrying into Cuban sugar connections. He later served as a major in the Civil War and died of typhoid in 1862. Dimock's racism, so intolerable today, would not have been uncommon to someone of his background and time. Dimock aggressively held the belief that Cuba's "manifest destiny" was to be annexed by the United States, and his *Travel Diary,* written in 1859, during an era of American expansionism, shows an undisguised belligerence towards all things Spanish. Following 1848 there were three raids by filibusters (pirates) to seize Cuba; as well as several offers made by the U.S. to buy Cuba from Spain, all without success.

Muir

John Muir (1838-1914) was one of the outstanding naturalists of his era. Born in Scotland, he lived in the United States after his parents emigrated to Wisconsin in 1849. Muir traveled extensively as a young man, visiting Cuba in 1868. As much a romantic as a scientist, he gives a breathless account of the natural wonders of the island. A visionary conservationist who might have been somewhat "before his time," Muir was a passionate advocate for the preservation and deeper understanding of nature.

Goodman

The English painter Walter Goodman's account of his Cuban adventures was published in 1873 under the title *The Pearl of the Antilles or An Artist in Cuba*. This book was one of a series of slightly off-beat (Goodman would have said "picturesque") travel guides from publishers Henry S. King, London.

Flint

Grover Flint was a former U.S. soldier who, in 1896, "covered" Cuba's Second War of Independence as a war correspondent. Flint rode with the insurgents for four months during their campaigns against the Spanish, and his book, *Marching with Gomez*, published in Boston in 1898, shows how rebel commanders such as Lacret were well versed in guerrilla warfare tactics.

Flint notes that: "*Gringo* is familiar to all who have lived in the Southwest as contemptuously applied by the Mexicans to Americans. It means something awkward and foreign. In Cuba I found it commonly applied to Spaniards."

Wright

Irene A. Wright (1879-1972) was an American journalist/editor who lived for 10 years in Cuba, working on what would today be called "trade publications" — writing, as she says, "from agricultural and industrial points of view." Wright's *Cuba* (1910) gives a detailed picture of the island's life in the first decade of the 20th century. In her foreword, she comments: "Cuba... has, very justly, it seems to me, been called the land of topsy-turvey. Here logic and rational sequence are not the rule. Life runs, not like reality, but after the style of librettos of stage plays. From largest to smallest, contradiction exists in all the details of our daily life. Here there are woods which sink and stones which float." Wright also wrote *The Early History of Cuba 1492-1586*, published in New York in 1916.

Nin

The well-known author of fiction, Anaïs Nin (1903–77), is equally famous for her voluminous *Diary*. Nin, the daughter of a French-Danish singer and Cuban musician and composer, was 19 when she visited Cuba for the first time in 1922. These extracts from Nin's *Early Diary* cover a period from October to November of that year.

Terry

Terry's Guide to Cuba, was one of a series of popular travel books by T. Phillip Terry written for well-heeled Americans in the 1920s and 1930s. Among the specially selected advertisements approved for the guide, is one for the Florida East Coast Railway, where a Cuba sea-rail excursion is described as part of the "American Riviera" tour, along with "such well-known resorts as St. Augustine, Ormond, Daytona Beach, the Palm Beaches and magical Miami." Reading Terry's pages, we can imagine Cuba in 1929 flooded with all manner of Americans, from pan-handling beach bums to cashed-up industrialists, to America's newly mobile middle class, all either seeking their fortunes or fashionable "flapper-era" pleasures amidst a tropical tourist paradise.

Hughes

The much-traveled black American diarist, novelist and poet Langston Hughes (1902-67) was 28 when he visited Cuba for the third time in 1930. "Cuban color lines," his experience of unforeseen color prejudice, appeared in 1956 in his book *I Wonder as I Wander: An Autobiographical Journey*. Reprinted by permission of Farrar, Strauss & Giroux.

Verrill

A. Hyatt Verrill was the author of a string of popular guides to Latin American destinations. In his *Cuba of Today*, published in 1931, he frankly cautions his fellow Americans: "I have yet to find the Latin American country whose people have any real love for the *Gringoes*... Not that I blame them. We... are beginning to learn... that the Latin Americans are not a lot of uncivilized, crude, semi-barbarous beings... over whose heads we can wave the "big stick" as if they were a crowd of unruly hoodlums. We may eventually learn to keep our hands off their private affairs and their politics, and we may some day learn to treat them like our equals."

Samuelson

Arnold Samuelson (1912-81) was a former farm boy and aspiring author for whom Hemingway became a role model, mentor and father figure. For about a year, Samuelson worked for "E.H." aboard the *Pilar* and the younger man's account of his adventures sailing with the master appeared in 1984 under the title of *With Hemingway: A Year In Key West and Cuba.*

Fergusson

Erna's Fergusson's *Cuba*, appeared in 1946. Written mainly for Americans, it was researched with help from the Cuban Tourist Commission. The Dr. Ortiz who Fergusson quotes here was the author, he says, of "a most useful book on Afro-Cuban rites," *Hampa Cubana, Los Negros Brujos (Cuban Underworld, Negro Witch Doctors).*

Fermor

Patrick Leigh Fermor, the well-known author of many outstanding books of travel literature, was in Havana for carnival in July 1949. His vivid and exhilarating account appeared in *The Traveler's Tree*, published in 1950.

Ragano and Raab

Frank Ragano was an attorney who provided legal services for Mafia heavyweights such as the Havana-based Santo Trafficante, who had interests in casinos and hotels before the revolution pushed him out. Trafficante found it convenient to remain on the island, where he could avoid questioning by American authorities. This required meeting his attorney in Havana. Ragano's first trip there had nothing to do with work. He had taken a holiday with his wife in 1956, but was shocked by the city's vice. On subsequent trips to see the mobster, the attorney travelled alone. Ragano's Cuba dealings were detailed in his 1994 autobiography, *Mob Lawyer*, written with New York reporter Selwyn Raab.

JOSE MARTI READER
Writings on the Americas
An outstanding new anthology of the writings, letters and poetry of one of the most important and brilliant Latin American voices of the 19th century. Teacher, journalist, revolutionary and poet, José Martí interweaves the threads of Latin American culture and history, condemning the brutality of the Spanish colonizers as well as the increasingly predatory ambitions of the United States in Latin America.
ISBN 1-875284-12-5

CUBAN REVOLUTION READER
A Documentary History
Edited by Julio García Luis
This Reader documents the development of the Cuban Revolution, one of the defining events of the 20th century, highlighting 40 key episodes over the past four decades. Introductory notes present the background and context of each document, article and speech.
ISBN 1-876175-10-9 *Also available in Spanish (ISBN 1-876175-28-1)*

CUBA AND THE UNITED STATES
A Chronological History
By Jane Franklin
This chronology relates in detail the developments involving the two neighboring countries from the 1959 revolution through 1995. An invaluable resource for scholars, teachers, journalists and legislators, offering an unprecedented vision of U.S.-Cuba relations.
ISBN 1-875284-92-3

MY EARLY YEARS
By Fidel Castro
Fidel Castro reflects on his childhood, youth and student days in an unprecedented and remarkably candid manner. Introductory essay by Gabriel García Márquez
ISBN 1-876175-07-9

CUBA — TALKING ABOUT REVOLUTION
Conversations with Juan Antonio Blanco by Medea Benjamin
One of Cuba's outstanding intellectuals discusses Cuba today, featuring an essay, "Cuba: 'socialist museum' or social laboratory?" A frank discussion on the current situation in Cuba.
ISBN 1-875284-97-4

IN THE SPIRIT OF WANDERING TEACHERS
The Cuban Literacy Campaign, 1961
A graphic record capturing the youthful spirit of the early years of the Cuban revolution. Text in English and Spanish. Photos.
ISBN 1-876175-39-7

HAVANA–MIAMI
The U.S.–Cuba migration conflict
By Jesús Arboleya
This book examines the origins of the migration conflict and why it has become such an important U.S. domestic issue.
ISBN 1-875284-91-5

THE MAFIA IN CUBA
The Cocaine and Casino Years
By Enrique Cirules

Dazzling Havana, the Mafia wars, crooked local politicians, "Lucky" Luciano and Meyer Lansky — these are all part of the vivid picture of the Mafia empire painted by Enrique Cirules, bringing this dark page of Cuban history alive. Cirules uses mountains of contemporary sources to reveal the amazing extent and depth to which the Mafia had penetrated almost every aspect of Cuban political, economic and social life.
ISBN 1-876175-42-7

CUBA: QUE BOLA!
A Photographic Essay
By Tania Jovanovic

"One person's encounter with a culture whose rhythms resonate in each image, sharing in a song of community, of zest, of life lived." The vitality of Cuba's people and the richness of the island's culture are captured by this outstanding photographic essay. A particular feature of Jovanovic's portraits are her images of Afro-Cuban culture and religion (santeria).
Includes both English and Spanish text.
ISBN 1-876175-20-6

AFROCUBA
An Anthology of Cuban Writing on Race, Politics and Culture
Edited by Pedro Pérez Sarduy and Jean Stubbs

What is it like to be Black in Cuba? Does racism exist in a revolutionary society that claims to have abolished it? *AfroCuba* looks at the Black experience through the eyes of the island's writers, scholars and artists.
ISBN 1-875284-41-9

Ocean Press
Australia: GPO Box 3279, Melbourne 3001, Australia
 •Fax: (61-3) 9329 5040
USA: PO Box 1186, Old Chelsea Stn., New York, NY 10113-1186
 •Tel: (1-718) 246 4160
E-mail: info@oceanbooks.com.au
www.oceanbooks.com.au